Literacy Is Not Enough

21st-Century Fluencies
for the Digital Age

21st Century Fluency Project

Lee Crockett

Lee Crockett is a national award-winning designer, artist, author, and international keynote speaker. He is the Managing Partner of The 21st Century Fluency Project and is co-author of *Understanding the Digital Generation*, *The Digital Diet*, *Living on the Future Edge*, and *Literacy Is Not Enough*. Lee is a "just in time" learner, constantly adapting to the new programs and technologies associated with today's communications and marketing media. Understanding the need for balance in our increasingly digital lives, Lee has lived in Kyoto, Japan, where he studied Aikido and Tea Ceremony, as well as Florence, Italy, where he studied painting.

Ian Jukes

Ian Jukes is The Committed Sardine: He has been a teacher at all grade levels; a school, district, and provincial administrator; a university instructor; and a national and international consultant. But first and foremost, Ian is a passionate educational evangelist. To date, he has written or co-written 14 books and 9 educational series and has had more than 200 articles published in various journals around the world. From the beginning, Ian's focus has been on the compelling need to restructure our educational institutions so that they become relevant to the current and future needs of children or, as David Thornburg writes, "to prepare them for their future and not just our past."

Andrew Churches

Andrew Churches is a teacher and ICT enthusiast. He teaches at Kristin School on Auckland's North Shore, a school with a mobile computing program that sees students with personal mobile devices and laptops. He is the co-author of *The Digital Diet* and *Apps for Learning*. He is an edublogger, wiki author, and innovator. In 2008, 2009, and 2010, Andrew's wiki, Educational Origami, was nominated for the Edublogs Best Wiki awards. Andrew was also a finalist in the Microsoft Distinguished Educators Awards in 2009. He contributes to a number of web sites and blogs, including Techlearning, *Spectrum Education* magazine, and the Committed Sardine blog. Andrew believes that to prepare our students for the future, we must prepare them for change and teach them to question, think, adapt, and modify.

We dedicate this book to the children of the 21st century. You are our future artists, innovators, scientists, and leaders. Our purpose is to help transform education to become relevant to life in the 21st century. Through our books, workshops, resources, and presentations, we strive constantly to speak on your behalf and to give you a voice. We are here to ensure that the education system that awaits you will be one that will help you cultivate the 21st-century fluencies essential for you to thrive in this time of exponential change—an education system that prepares you for your future and not our past.

21st Century Fluency Project

co-published with

CORWIN
A SAGE Company

Cover photos and illustrations: © iStockphoto.com, © 21st Century Fluency Project Inc.
Copyright © 2011 by 21st Century Fluency Project Inc.
Page 35: Image from DHMO.org reprinted with permisssion.
Page 43: Quote by Daniel Pink (*A Whole New Mind*, 2005, pg. 54) reprinted with permission.

For information:
21st Century Fluency Project Inc.
778-938-2100
www.fluency21.com

ISBN-13: 9781412987806

Acquisitions Editor: Debra Stollenwerk
Editorial, Production, and Indexing: Abella Publishing Services, LLC
Typesetter: Ross Crockett
Graphic Design: Lee Crockett

Disclaimer
Every attempt has been made to contact known copyright holders included in this work. Any errors are unintended and should be brought to the attention of the publisher for corrections in subsequent printings.

 Table of Contents

21st Century Fluency Project

The 21st Century Fluency Project is about moving vision into practice through the process of investigating the impact of change on our society and our children over the past few decades, learning how educators of today must evolve, and finally, commit to changes at the classroom level.

Literacy Is Not Enough is the fourth book in our 21st-Century Fluency Series. We face a world on the move, and education needs to react. A series of six books, as well as related supporting materials, has been developed to answer five essential questions that teachers will ask when considering how educators and education must respond to the profound developments being experienced in the world at large.

Why Do I Have to Change?

Living on the Future Edge

Windows on Tomorrow

In this book, we discuss the power of paradigm to shape our thinking, the pressures that technological development is putting on our paradigm for teaching and learning, six exponential trends in technological development that we can't ignore, what these trends mean for education, new skills for students, new roles for teachers, and scenarios of education in the future.

Understanding the Digital Generation

Teaching and Learning in the New Digital Landscape

This book examines the effects that digital bombardment from constant exposure to electronic media has on students in the new digital landscape and considers the profound implications this holds for the future of education. What does the latest neuroscientific and psychological research tell us about the role of intense and frequent experiences on the brain, particularly the young and impressionable brain?

Based on the research, what inferences can we make about kids' digital experiences and how these experiences are rewiring and reshaping their cognitive processes? More important, what are the implications for teaching, learning, and assessment in the new digital landscape?

How can we reconcile these new developments with current instructional practices, particularly in a climate of standards and accountability driven by high-stakes testing for all? What strategies can we use to appeal to the learning preferences and communication needs of digital learners while honoring our traditional assumptions and practices related to teaching, learning, and assessment?

Where Do I Start?

The Digital Diet
Today's Digital Tools in Small Bytes

This book offers bite-sized, progressively challenging projects to introduce the reader to the digital landscape of today. This is the world of our children and students. The Digital Diet will help readers shed pounds of assumptions and boost their digital metabolism to help keep pace with these kids by learning to use some simple yet powerful digital tools.

What Would This Teaching Look Like in My Classroom?

Literacy Is Not Enough
21st-Century Fluencies for the Digital Age

It is no longer enough to educate only to the standards of traditional literacies. To be competent and capable in the 21st century requires a completely different set of skills—the 21st-century fluencies—that are identified and explained in detail in this book. The balance of the book introduces our framework for integrating these fluencies in our traditional curriculum.

21st-Century Fluency Kits

These kits are subject- and grade-specific publications designed to integrate the teaching of 21st-century fluencies into today's curriculum and classroom. Included are detailed learning scenarios, resources, rubrics, and lesson plans with suggestions for high-tech, low-tech, or no-tech implementation. Also identified is the traditional content covered, as well as the standards and 21st-century fluencies each project covers.

Apps For Learning
40 Best iPad/iPhone/iPod Touch Apps

In the classroom of the 21st century, the power of mobility has begun to play a significant role in the learning experiences of our students. The ubiquitous digital devices they use so frequently and unconsciously can be harnessed as powerful tools for learning, creativity, and discovery. And, as the saying goes, "there's an app for that."

This remarkable and revealing three-book series on the best choices for learning apps in the classroom covers mobility apps categories for utilities, general classroom applications, and also specialty apps designed with unique learning tools that students can utilize both in class and on the go. Each book is devoted to a specific grade level—one for elementary school, middle school, and high school.

The *Apps For Learning* books will show how both you and students can get the most out of our versatile mobile technology and turn the classroom into a personal digital adventure in learning.

The 21st Century Fluency Project Web Site
www.fluency21.com

Our web site contains supplemental material that provides support for classroom teachers who are implementing 21st-century teaching. The site lets teachers access premade lesson plans that teach traditional content along with 21st-century fluencies. The site also provides teachers with a blank template for designing their own lessons for teaching 21st-century fluencies. There are also other shared resources and a forum for additional collaboration and support.

How Can We Design Effective Schools for the 21st Century?

Teaching the Digital Generation

No More Cookie-Cutter High Schools

The world has changed. Young people have changed. But the same underlying assumptions about teachers, students, and instruction that have guided high school design for a hundred years continue to shape the way high schools are designed today. In fact, so much is assumed about the way a high school should look that new schools are created from a long-established template without question. Strip away the skylights, the fancy foyers, and the high-tech PA systems, and new schools being constructed today look pretty much the way they did when most adults went to school.

This is a mismatch with reality. We need new designs that incorporate what we have learned about young people and how they learn best. This book outlines a new process for designing high schools and provides descriptions of several new models for how schools can be configured to better support learning.

# Introduction

It is no longer enough that we educate only to the standards of the traditional literacies. If students are to survive, let alone thrive, in the 21st-century culture of technology-driven automation, abundance, and access to global labor markets, then independent thinking and its corollary, creative thinking, hold the highest currency. To be competent and capable in the 21st century requires a completely different set of skills. These 21st-century fluencies (Solution Fluency, Information Fluency, Creativity Fluency, Media Fluency, Collaboration Fluency, and Global Digital Citizenship) are identified and explained in detail in this book as processes that can be learned and applied by students.

The book goes further by identifying the 21st-century learning environment and detailing the process for developing scenarios and unit plans that address traditional curriculum while cultivating these essential fluencies. As a departure from most other books available on the subject today, we go beyond the "why" we need to change and focuses on the "how" to change. In our presentations and workshops around the world, we are finding there is a reasonably good understanding of why we need to change, and educators would like to hear about how to change. That's what *Literacy Is Not Enough* is about.

Today, we face a different kind of student. Technological changes are altering the minds of our children, both physically and chemically, which is changing their learning styles and preferences. Our children are not the same as we were growing up, and they are not the students our teachers were trained to teach or that our schools are designed for.

As we follow the fluencies, we will have a brief discussion of what learning looks like in a 21st-century environment. This leads us to the main part of the book, which is a detailed guide to transforming your classroom to be relevant to students while addressing the standards and, at the same time, cultivating the 21st-century fluencies. We will walk you through the process and provide you with examples we use in our workshops and in our own unit plan writing. Several samples of complete units and the template for developing your own are included at the end of this book.

Before we get to work, we'd like to share this poem with you. It really sums up what we believe and what we strive to achieve in our work.

What Is a Teacher?

What is a teacher?

A guide, not a guard.

What is learning?

A journey, not a destination.

What is discovery?

Questioning the answers, not answering the questions.

What is the process?

Discovering ideas, not covering content.

What is the goal?

Open minds, not closed issues.

What is the test?
Being and becoming, not remembering and reviewing.

What is learning?
Not just doing things differently, but doing different things.

What is teaching?
Not showing them what to learn, but showing them how to learn.

What is school?
Whatever we choose to make it.

—**Allan Glatthorn**

Chapter 1
Highly Educated, Useless People

> Education has produced a vast population able to read but unable to distinguish what is worth reading.
>
> G. M. Trevelyan

A few years ago, we were asked to speak at an international educational conference. Shortly after our presentation, we heard the commentator, the minister of education from a certain high-profile country, make the following statement: "Our students are amongst the very best performers academically in the world on the TIMS." (TIMS stands for the Third International Mathematics and Science Study.)

He then added, "The problem is that most of them couldn't think their way out of a wet paper bag if their life depended upon it. They're nothing but highly educated, useless people."

We were speechless. Highly educated, useless people?

What was he really telling us?

What he was saying was that his high-achieving students had school smarts and thus could excel at school-related activities. They had developed special abilities that would allow them to move smoothly through the school system because they had developed the necessary skills to effectively cram for tests and write the answers. What he was suggesting was that most academically successful students do well in large part because they have learned to play and excel at a game called school.

But in describing them as "highly educated, useless people," what he was also suggesting was that many students in his country, particularly the brainy ones with school smarts, did not possess what is generally known as street smarts. For him, being street-smart was about students having higher-level thinking skills and competencies that would allow them to go above and beyond success on written exams and enable them to live and work in the real world beyond school, solving real-life problems in real time.

We became curious: What was the difference between being school-smart and street-smart? What would make so many of these students, who were good at school and able to do well on tests, at the same time inadequately prepared for life? What was going on?

After much debate about our expectations of school learning and how to accomplish it, we believe we finally have one answer. This answer is related to how we teach our students to learn and think.

When children first attend primary school, they depend on their teachers to tell them what they need to do, how to do it, when to do it, where to sit when they are doing it, and even how long to sit. Their primary focus in school becomes more and more about mastering content and learning through memorization in a tightly controlled instructional environment.

In this world, mastery of content is valued over thinking critically about the content. Teachers tell their students what they need to do to pass the test, to pass the course, to pass the grade, to move to the next level, and finally to graduate.

All the answers are prearranged, preformatted, and ready for absorption by those who are willing and able to play the game called school. These are the academically successful. They are the students who are comfortable operating in a culture of dependency—dependent on the teacher, the textbook, and the test.

Then, after having spent 13 or more years in the system, our students graduate from school, and the educational infrastructure that has held them up for all their years in education is suddenly removed. When this happens, many of the students fall flat on their faces as they enter the real world. And we can't understand why, even though it is we, the educators, who were responsible for creating this culture of dependence in the first place.

Progressive Withdrawal

Today, success in school clearly does not guarantee success in life. So what is the problem? The answer lies in our efforts to ensure compliance in our learners. Somewhere along the line, we have lost sight of the need to develop in our students the capacity to become independent thinkers and doers.

If our students are to survive, let alone thrive, in the 21st-century culture of technology-driven automation, abundance, and access to global labor markets, then independent thinking and its corollary, creative thinking, hold the highest currency.

To help our students make a successful transition from school to life, we must shift the responsibility of learning from the teacher, where it has traditionally been, to the learners, where it belongs. Our job as educators will be to move from demanding the compliance of our students to making ourselves progressively redundant.

Although this may sound simple, it is, in fact, an incredibly complex task. For this change to occur and be truly successful, it must be accepted into the hearts and minds of every educational stakeholder: politicians, policy designers, administrators, teachers, parents, and even the students. The new and different paradigm of teaching and learning is that of progressive withdrawal. Our responsibility must be to ensure that our students no longer need us by the time they graduate from school.

This is no different than what we do as parents. Think back to the very first tentative steps of your children. They stood there wobbling and teetering, and inevitably they fell down. What did you do when this happened? Did you rush over, point at them, and say, "39—you fail" or "Oh, well, I'd rate that as 28 percent. That was a C minus. I'm sorry, you've had five chances; you don't get any more." The answer is—of course not! What we did was clap our hands, help them up, brush them off, wipe away their tears, and encourage them to try again. That was, we understood, our job as parents.

As difficult and challenging as it might be, particularly during our children's teenage years, our responsibility is still to help them become independent people who can stand on their own as they begin to make their way through life.

So what should we do? Do we give up on helping our students to become school-smart and simply focus on helping them become street-smart? Absolutely not! We need them to be both school-smart and street-smart. This is not a matter of either/or.

Moving Toward 21st-Century Learning

We need to ask some deeper questions. For example, what do we want our students to become? What do we want them to feel and think? And what must they do to measurably demonstrate their preparation and willingness to leave school and go into the world to work, live, and play?

These are not easy questions to answer. We live in the dynamic world of InfoWhelm, where content is growing exponentially in both quantity and complexity. In this shifting landscape, where digital content is readily available at our fingertips, learners must be able to move beyond mastery of content recall. Bubble tests will not get them the tools they need to achieve success in the world for which they are preparing. Their success in work, life, and play will greatly depend on their ability to interpret and apply old information and new alike to new situations, problems, and environments.

Access to information is not the issue. Information is in constant flux and readily available. Rather, learners must become discerning and creative consumers of information. In this new digital reality, the application of higher-order thinking and independent cognitive skills in the context of real-world, real-life, and real-time tasks is of critical importance. Our students must transfer previous learning to new situations and different challenges.

We firmly believe that invoking progressive withdrawal and fostering street smarts in school-smart students requires a major shift in the existing educational paradigm. This shift demands that we rethink the design of our schools, our classrooms, and our learning environments.

At the same time, we need to rethink our assumptions about instructional design, what constitutes learning, and even what it means to be intelligent. Ultimately, we must also rethink how we assess and evaluate effective instruction and effective learning. The exponentially growing body of content due to InfoWhelm has moved beyond traditional school subjects and into newer 21st-century content areas of global awareness; financial, economic, business, and entrepreneurial literacy; civic literacy; health and wellness awareness; leadership; ethics; and accountability. The list keeps growing. To become independent learners requires the development of two types of skills: those that emerge from the critical cognitive intelligences and those that come from emotional intelligence.

Cognitive Intelligence

These competencies primarily involve rational higher-order thinking skills. These skills include how to manage, interpret, validate, transform, communicate, and act on information. Cognitive intelligence includes abstract reasoning, problem solving, communications, creativity, innovation, contextualized learning, technical information, and media fluency skills all used in the context of content areas.

Emotional Intelligence

There are four major skill sets that comprise emotional intelligence. They are self-awareness, self-management, social awareness, and relationship management.

Today, there is much evidence to show that significant leverage can be obtained by promoting learning strategies in emotional intelligence. Emotional intelligence is particularly important in developing street smarts.

It's ridiculous to continue to embrace standardized learning and standardized tests at the very same time our new economy is eliminating standardized jobs.

Assessing Learning

Let's not forget the matter of what we assess and how we assess learning. Standardized tests, such as bubble tests and fill-in-the-blanks exams, cover only a narrow range of rational cognitive skills. Real learning is about much more than this.

Five Fundamental Changes

The bottom line is that schools must change drastically if we are to reverse the growing disconnect between being school-smart and being street-smart. If we are going to develop schools that are more relevant to our students' futures—if we are going to prepare students for the real world that awaits them—we must make at least five fundamental changes.

1. Acknowledge the new digital landscape—Schools must embrace the new digital reality of the online, computerized world Friedman describes in *The World Is Flat* (Friedman, 2005). Outside of schools, the digital world has fundamentally and irrevocably altered the way things get done. This is the case not just for business but also for many aspects of our lives.

It must be stressed that this is not about schools having high-speed networks or students being able to use tablets, laptops, or handhelds. If high-tech resources are available but are used only to reinforce old mindsets and assumptions about teaching, learning, and how learning is assessed, little will have changed. Transforming education is about developing the full spectrum of cognitive and emotional intelligences that are increasingly required in our 21st-century culture. As such, this is primarily a *headware* or mindset issue, not a hardware issue.

2. Provide guidance as well as access—The new digital landscape allows students to access information and learning experiences outside schools and classrooms. Learners can engage in experiences that have traditionally been the domain of teachers and the adult world. From home, a car, or the shopping mall, whenever and wherever they are, students can access information, music, original sources, and multimedia, full-motion color video from friends and acquaintances, as well as from people who might hold perspectives diametrically opposed to theirs. However, because of our current fixation on testing, we are unable to properly guide our students or help them develop the skills that will empower them to effectively use and communicate with these powerful tools. As a result, it is often the students, not the teachers, who define where they go, how they get there, and what they do when they arrive.

Compounded by the fact that many adults, decision makers, and educators are not in sync with the new digital reality of our students, we don't have the experience, the skills, or even the inclination to help them when we have the time. Schools and teachers persist in using new tools to reinforce old mindsets about what is learned, how it is learned, and how that learning is assessed.

To understand the new digital landscape—to leverage our students' world—we must be willing to immerse ourselves in that world and embrace the new digital reality. If we can't relate, if we don't "get it," we won't be able to make schools relevant to the current and future needs of the digital generation.

3. Change minds—We must address the shift in thinking patterns that is happening to the digital generation. They live and operate in a multimedia, online, multitask, random access, color graphics, video, audio, visual world.

As Steven Johnson points out in his book, *Everything Bad Is Good for You* (2005), these new skills are not generally acknowledged, valued, or addressed in our schools. This is because these emerging competencies do not generally reflect our traditional definitions of literacy, which were confined and defined by the technologies of the 19th and 20th centuries when tablets, PCs, the Internet, cell phones, and other types of digital technologies were the stuff of science fiction.

We must acknowledge that because of this new digital landscape, our students not only think differently but also learn differently from the way we learn. Only by accepting this can we begin to reconsider and redesign learning environments, instruction, and how we assess learning.

4. Teach the whole learner—We must broaden evaluation to encompass activities that provide a complete picture of student learning. As management guru Tom Peters says, "What gets measured gets done," and conversely, "what doesn't get measured doesn't get done."

It's imperative that we begin to measure more than just information recall. Dave Masters uses this analogy:

> "You can get a good picture of a person's health by taking their height and weight. But would you go to a doctor who only took your height and weight and said here's a picture of your health? The answer of course is no. It would require a battery of tests—blood tests, blood pressure, urinalysis, cholesterol, checking for lumps, and so on to get an accurate picture of your health."

Schools test students using standardized instruments that primarily measure information recall and low-level understanding and then consider the results a complete picture of their students' learning. This is absolutely not accurate. It is extremely presumptuous for us to say that current test scores are adequate indicators of student learning. A picture of student learning must include a portfolio of performance, demonstrations of the student's learning, and the application of theories to solve real-world problems.

Our school system wrongly assumes that every brain is the same by ignoring the fact that every brain is wired differently. Children do not all look alike, and they do not all learn the same way either. But since most children are taught the same way, it follows that some will fail. It's ridiculous to continue to embrace standardized learning and standardized tests as the only ways to assess learning. At the very same time, our new economy is eliminating standardized jobs. If there's one certainty about what today's schoolchildren will be doing a decade or two from now, it's that they won't all be doing the same thing and they certainly won't be drawing on the same body of knowledge. That's why education has to change.

5. Emphasize relevancy and connections—Last, but not least, we must elevate the connection between instruction in school and the world outside if we hope to increase the relevancy of the learning that takes place. The key point here is that students must perceive the relevancy of what they're learning. They need to understand not just the content but also the context of that content as it applies to the world outside of school.

For this to happen, schools need to become less insular. Administrators, teachers, parents, and students must work systematically to bring the outside world into the classroom while sending our students out into the community. New technologies and an understanding of the new digital landscape can help us do both. The online world creates virtual highways and virtual hallways to local and global communities.

Achieving Street Smarts and School Smarts

To unfold the full intellectual and creative genius of all of our children—to prepare them for their future, not the past—we must provide relevant 21st-century skills, which can form a bridge between their world and ours. This is key to developing both street smarts and school smarts.

We must look for alternatives to the traditional organization of schools. We need to uncover our long-standing and unexamined assumptions about teaching and learning, about what a classroom looks like, where learning takes place, and the resources needed to support it.

We also need to re-examine our use of time—the length of the school day and school year, the school timetable, and the traditional methods used for instructional delivery. And we must consider the potential of online, web-based, virtual learning that can be used to augment, extend, and transform the role of the traditional classroom teacher.

In other words, we cannot foster street smarts in students who are school-smart until we answer some powerful and relevant questions about our assumptions of what schools currently are and what they need to be.

Summarizing the Main Points

- If our students are to survive, let alone thrive, in the 21st-century culture of technology-driven automation, abundance, and access to global labor markets, then independent thinking and its corollary, creative thinking, hold the highest currency.

- The new and different paradigm of teaching and learning is that of progressive withdrawal. Our responsibility must be to ensure that our students no longer need us by the time they graduate from school.

- Learners must be able to move beyond mastery of content recall. Their success in work, life, and play will greatly depend on their ability to interpret and apply old information and new alike to new situations, problems, and environments.

- To become independent learners requires the development of two types of skills: those that emerge from the critical cognitive intelligences and those that come from emotional intelligence.

- Transforming education is about developing the full spectrum of cognitive and emotional intelligences that are increasingly required in the culture of the 21st century. As such, this is primarily a headware or mindset issue, not a hardware issue.

- To understand the new digital landscape—to leverage our students' world— we must be willing to immerse ourselves in that world and embrace the new digital reality.

- We must acknowledge that because of this new digital landscape, our students not only think differently but also learn differently from the way we learn.

- A picture of student learning must include a portfolio of performance, demonstrations of the student's learning, and the application of theories to solve real-world problems.

- Students must perceive the relevancy of what they're learning. They need to understand not just the content but also the context of that content as it applies to the world outside of school.

Questions to Consider

- What does the phrase "highly educated, useless people" mean to you?

- How do we currently teach our children to learn and to think, and how does it need to change?

- What must our children do to measurably demonstrate their preparation and readiness to leave school and go into the world to work, live, and play?

- What are our assumptions about instructional design, what constitutes learning, and what it means to be intelligent?

Chapter 2

Is the Factory Gone?

50,000 factories closed in the U.S. in the past 20 years.

Congressman Bernie Sanders (*The Daily Show With Jon Stewart*, April 28, 2011)

Technology changes everything. Consider how the telephone, radio, television, and most recently the Internet have made our world a much smaller place. As new technologies and the global transportation infrastructure have grown, corporations have opted for easier, faster, and more economical ways to produce products overseas. The result, however, has been the nearly complete disappearance of factory jobs in the United States.

Deindustrialization has been going on for decades. At one time, this trend was a major concern for us. But the realities of the marketplace today seem to make sense to the average consumer. Everyone understands that it's cheaper to manufacture overseas, even if it means shipping raw materials halfway around the world, where they are assembled and returned as finished products. "Made in China, sold at Wal-Mart" is something we've come to accept.

The Life and Death of the American Factory

But how does this look in your own backyard? The *New York Times* reported the following on June 19, 2010:

> "Having seen her father make a solid living at the Whirlpool refrigerator factory, Natalie Ford was enthusiastic about landing a job there and was happy years later when her 20-year-old son also went to work there.

> But that family tradition will soon end because Whirlpool plans to close the plant on Friday and move the operation to Mexico, eliminating 1,100 jobs here. Many in this city in southern Indiana are seething and sad—sad about losing what was long the city's economic centerpiece and a ticket to the middle class for one generation after another.

> "This is all about corporate greed," said Ms. Ford, who took a job at Whirlpool 19 years ago. "It's devastating to our family and to everyone in the plant. I wonder where we'll be two years or four years from now. There aren't any jobs here. How is this community going to survive?"

> At a time when the nation's economy is struggling to gain momentum, Whirlpool's decision is an unwelcome step backward. It continues a trend in which the nation has lost nearly six million factory jobs over the past dozen years, representing one in three manufacturing jobs."

Consider that six million factory jobs over the past dozen years are gone and are not coming back. The pace of factories disappearing has not slowed down, stalled, or halted. Big companies with big factories all across the country are shutting their doors: Chrysler's engine factory in Kenosha, WI; Perfect Fit Industries' textile factory in Loogootee, IN; and the Quad/Graphics, Inc., printing facilities in Dyersburge, TN, Reno, NV, Clarksville, TN, Levanon, OH, and Corinth, MS. (Esinger, 2010)

The Old World of Work

Former president Woodrow Wilson said this about public education: "We want one class of persons to have a liberal education, and we want another class of persons, a very much larger class, of necessity, in every society, to forgo the privileges of liberal education and fit themselves to perform specific and difficult manual tasks."

Reflected in this statement is the great promise of a liberal education and the American Dream. A select few went on to higher education and distinguished professional careers. For those who didn't, a relatively stable job that paid well was to be had at the factory just down the street. You didn't need a college degree or even a high school education. All you needed was a strong back and a few basic skills. You could quit school and, by the end of the week, be trained and working.

Those who focused on getting a better education believed that it would translate into a better job. Having a degree was seen as the key to the future. We were told that if we studied hard, if we received good grades, if we went to the right universities, and if we got our degrees, great jobs and unlimited opportunities awaited us. But is this still true today?

The Death of Distance

White-collar jobs were desirable, but in reality, they were still just factory positions. It makes no difference whether you're twisting a wrench or pushing a pencil. It's still routine cognitive work; your hands just don't get as dirty. And herein lies the problem. Routine cognitive work is being outsourced constantly: tax preparers, bookkeepers, data-entry clerks, computer programmers, legal researchers, call-center workers, receptionists, and personal assistants, to name just a few, are today seeing their jobs outsourced. What these jobs have in common is that they involve repetitive, routine mental tasks. The people who perform them do not have to be local.

Global interconnectedness through electronic means has meant the death of distance. Just as factory jobs can be outsourced to where labor is cheaper, in a wired world, it makes no difference if you send documents to the third floor or the Third World—it takes about the same amount of time for them to arrive, which is pretty much instantaneously.

Even people who interpret MRIs and X-rays are doing routine cognitive work. Would it surprise you to know that an MRI done in Chicago was analyzed by a technician in Asia and the results were sent to your doctor in the time it took you to drive to his office?

Savvy employers now assemble virtual global work teams on a project-by-project basis. For example, more than 5 million private contractors around the world, in every imaginable work category, from designers and writers to data-entry clerks and programmers, are connected with employers through oDesk, one of many online services that assist in this process. Many can be hired for a fraction of what it costs to hire an employee in the United States. Just place a job posting, and within minutes, you'll receive responses from dozens of qualified applicants. Each one has an extensive work history, work samples, and feedback from other jobs in the system. And there's no need to check references; you can just check feedback. The system tracks a contractor's work, counting mouse movements and keyboard strokes and taking a screen shot every 10 minutes. If your employees aren't working, you'll know it. Imagine the resistance to putting a system of accountability like that in the modern American office.

Hiring, on a project-by-project basis, someone who wants the job and is willing to do it for a fraction of what it would cost to hire someone locally seems pretty attractive to employers. No labor disputes, no tax deductions, no benefits, no vacations to work around, no perks—just results. Some people may call this outsourcing, but many call it the new way to do business. You may not like it, but it's absolutely the reality of the workplace. And as a result, millions of jobs are disappearing, primarily because technology allows a company to send work overseas. Just as in manufacturing, people elsewhere will do routine cognitive work for much less than it costs to get workers to do it in the United States.

In March 2011, $16,530,216 was earned by oDesk contractors logging more than 1.6 million hours (http://www.odesk.com/oconomy/). More than 89 percent of work performed online is for employers outside a worker's home country (http://www.odesk.com/blog/2011/04/international-payments-made-easy/), and oDesk is just one of many such services.

Work in a New World

The bottom line is that if work can be outsourced or sent offshore, it absolutely will be. If it can be automated, it will be. If it can be turned into software, it will be. In an increasingly global economy, this is the only way businesses can stay competitive. Routine cognitive work, like manufacturing, can be done almost anywhere—it's no longer locationally dependent.

What we are seeing is the outsourcing of pretty much everything. As a result, the once great educational truth about staying in school to get a good job has become the great educational lie. No longer is a degree a guarantee of a good job. When employers have the choice of hiring someone else, equally qualified, without hassles or long-term commitment and for a fraction of the cost, whom do you think they'll choose? Whom would you choose?

Creativity—The New Essential

To stay competitive in this new global economy, we need to shift our instructional approach to a 21st-century learning environment that will provide our students with the most in-demand skills; those that can't be easily outsourced, automated, or turned into software: creativity, lateral thinking, and problem solving dealing with nonroutine cognitive tasks.

In his book *The Rise of the Creative Class*, Richard Florida (2003) says you can divide the workforce into four basic groups: the agricultural class, the working class, the service class, and the creative class.

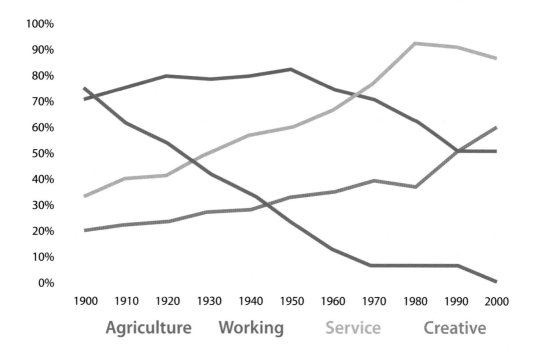

Agricultural class—In 1900, almost 40 percent of workers were employed in agriculture. Of course, back then, most of this work was done manually, by people and animals working long hours. Over the years, machines have slowly been replacing people, making farming more efficient. Today, agriculture represents less than 2 percent of the workforce. What used to be done by dozens of workers and animals can now be done with one worker with a single machine. In fact, in some cases, the worker isn't even required anymore. Have you seen those lawnmowers, the ones that park themselves in a little docking station after they motor around the lawn by themselves? Did you know there are tractors that can do the same thing, using the same technology? On a smaller scale, a robot can clean your floors, your pool, or your gutters.

Working class—This group includes the classic manufacturing workers, whose jobs require basic skills to perform. These jobs peaked right after World War II and have been steadily declining ever since. We've already discussed the reasons for this and the corresponding decline in manufacturing, extensively. There will always be working-class jobs, but the jobs that are insulated from globalization are primarily location dependent, such as the building trades, for example.

Service class—The service class includes location-dependent workers, the service industries or helping professions, and routine cognitive workers. These jobs peaked in 1980 and have been steadily shrinking ever since. Why? The answer is because of the growing power of personal computers. We alluded to the fact that routine cognitive work is being outsourced, but it's also being automated. Think about this for a moment: Every time you use a piece of software to do your taxes, and every time you use your computer to book a hotel, a flight, a car rental, or a concert ticket, you have done so without interacting with another human being. If you buy mutual funds, trade stocks, or do your banking online, you have cast a ballot and voted to have someone's job replaced. It sounds dramatic, but really, this is exactly what's happening.

Of course, these online services are convenient, and we are certainly not suggesting that you not use them; we are only pointing out why jobs are disappearing. Jobs that can be automated or turned into software will be. Some jobs can also be outsourced easily. That is why this sector of the workforce has been disappearing for 30 years, and there is no indication that this trend will be reversed.

Creative class—The creative class includes people who do nonroutine cognitive work and apply 21st-century skills, abstract and higher-level thinking, on a regular basis. Interestingly, you'll notice that the point at which the service class started to shrink is the exact moment that the creative class started to grow. It's not a subtle change in the graph, either, but a sharp reversal. The reason is the same for both groups: the personal computer had become affordable to the masses. However, unlike service-class jobs, creative-class jobs are facilitated by technology, not replaced by it.

With the obvious exception of location-dependent workers, the service class is rapidly disappearing. So to determine your vulnerability or the vulnerability of future generations, ask yourself if the computer can do your job faster or if someone living somewhere else can do your job for less. If the answer is yes, there is a high probability that your job is disappearing and that it will be gone in the future. It's simply global economics.

Literacy Is Not Enough

It is our job, as parents and as educators, to prepare our children and students for their life beyond school. If they are to be successful, it is critically important that we prepare them for the world that awaits them. However, our schools are not designed this way. Often, all it takes for students to do well in school is the ability to cram information and memorize facts to be regurgitated on exams and forgotten immediately after. We call it informational bulimia, and it is a long-standing academic tradition—it's how we play the game called school.

We are not being truthful when we assure students and their parents that mastering the state standards will give students all they need to be prepared for the rest of their lives. For example, Bob Marzano's research tells us that 80 to 85 percent of the work that kids do in their classes is focused on factual recall and lower-level thinking procedures. The routine cognitive work that depends on these skills, however, is increasingly disappearing or being outsourced.

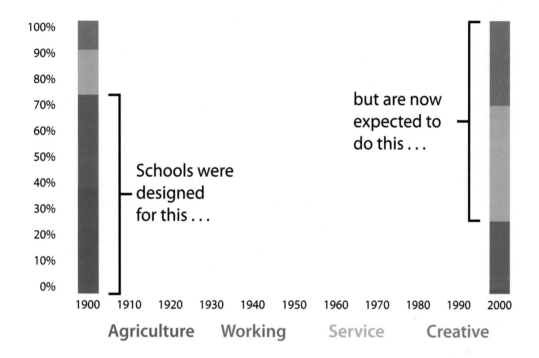

Our schools were designed for an era in which three-quarters of the population were employed in agriculture and manufacturing jobs. Those times are gone forever, but our educational institutions still embrace traditional structures, traditional organization, traditional instruction, standardized learning, and standardized testing at the same time that our economy is eliminating standardized jobs.

Today, three-quarters of our workforce are working in creative-class and service-class professions. If we want our students to survive, let alone thrive, in the culture and the workplace of the 21st century, literacy is not enough. It is critical that our students develop 21st-century skills. In fact, we would go so far as to say that these skills are more important than most of the traditional content taught in the curriculum today.

Literacy Versus Fluency

We want to take a moment to make an important distinction. It's actually our mindsets that we need to shift. There is a reason we use the term *21st-century fluencies* and not *21st-century literacy* or *21st-century skills*. Think about the difference between these terms.

When we are at the level of literacy with a language, we are able to communicate. However, our focus is on the structure of the language, on the translation, on the pronunciation, and on getting the words out. When we are fluent with a language, the concepts flow from our brain and out of our mouths. The process is transparent to us.

Our focus is on our thinking of what we want to say and not on the translation or the pronunciation. As a result, we are much more effective at expressing our true intention.

The same holds true for children who are learning to write. Their focus is on forming letters and using the tools of pencil and paper. But as we grow older and use these tools every day, the tools and the process become irrelevant. Our thoughts go directly from our minds through the tool, whether pencil or keyboard, to the medium.

The literacy level does not contain the fundamental skills our students need for their life beyond school. We need to raise the bar. Our goal should be the fluency level—the level at which these skills have become internalized to the point of transparency, where the skills become part of the unconscious process and do not stand in the way.

Change Is Hard—You Go First!

We look at educators of today as leaders. They must take risks and embrace a new pedagogy. The model of 21st-century learning calls for learners to get involved and get their hands dirty. They must be expected to go beyond the textbook to create real-world solutions to real-world problems. This takes a teacher willing to let go of the illusion of control and become a facilitator of learning, not a guardian of knowledge.

You are that educator, and it's you who has the ability to change what goes on in your classroom. You are already willing to make the shift; otherwise, you wouldn't be reading this book. Most likely, you understand why so much has been written on "why education needs to change," but what's lacking is the "how." Our goal is to assist you in making your classroom a 21st-century learning environment. How can we talk seriously about 21st-century skills for kids if we're not talking 21st-century skills for educators, too? In the coming chapters, we look at what the 21st-century fluencies are and how you can cultivate them in your students while addressing the curricular objectives.

Summarizing the Main Points

- Six million factory jobs over the past dozen years are gone and they are not coming back. The pace of factories disappearing has not slowed down, stalled, or halted.

- Routine cognitive work is being outsourced constantly. Savvy employers now assemble virtual global work teams on a project-by-project basis.

- To stay competitive in this new global economy, we need to shift our instructional approach to a 21st-century learning environment that will provide our students with the most in-demand skills, those that can't be easily outsourced, automated, or turned into software: creativity, lateral thinking, and problem solving dealing with nonroutine cognitive tasks.

- Our schools were designed for an era in which three-quarters of the population were employed in agriculture and manufacturing jobs.

- Our goal should be the fluency level—the level at which these skills have become internalized to the point of transparency, where the skills become part of the unconscious process and do not stand in the way.

- Educators must take risks and embrace a new pedagogy, go beyond the textbook to create real-world solutions to real-world problems, and to let go of the illusion of control and become a facilitator of learning.

Questions to Consider

- In what ways were our schools designed for an era in which three-quarters of the population were employed in agriculture and manufacturing jobs?

- What is the primary difference between literacy and fluency, and why is it important to consider in regards to our children's educational structuring?

- What does it mean to be a "facilitator of learning" instead of a "guardian of knowledge"?

solution fluency

information fluency

global digital citizen

creativity fluency

media fluency

collaboration fluency

Chapter 3
21st-Century Fluencies

> **The illiterate of the 21st century will not be those who cannot read and write, but those who cannot learn, unlearn, and relearn.**
>
> Alvin Toffler

We need to move our thinking and our training beyond our primary focus and fixation on the Three Rs—beyond traditional literacy to an additional set of 21st-century fluencies, skills that reflect the times we live in.

How we learn reading, writing, and mathematics has changed. In the age of multimedia, hypertext, blogs, and wikis, reading is no longer just a passive, linear activity that deals only with text, with reading literature, manuals, workbooks, computer screens, or technical instructions. At the same time, writing has also changed and is no longer just about being able to communicate effectively with pen, paper, and text. Writing has moved beyond just creating traditional reports, filling out forms, or making written instructions. Math is about more than simply memorizing and applying formulae, definitions, and algorithms.

Today, it's essential that all of our students have a wide range of skills beyond those that were needed in the 20th century, a range that includes the skills needed to function within a rapidly changing society. In the process of outlining what these new skills are, we have identified five skill categories. These following classifications were originally developed by Ted McCain and Ian Jukes as part of their keynote presentation *Understanding the Digital Generation Part II: Strategies That Work* (2009).

The Five Skill Categories

Obsolete Skills

Obsolete skills are traditional skills that were once valued but are no longer. They are not bad skills—they're just no longer as important or relevant to the world and to the times we live in. Some examples of obsolete skills are shoeing horses, sharpening swords, running an elevator, making candles, and setting type. There's nothing wrong with these skills, but except for a small minority of people in our communities, they are obsolete.

Traditional Skills

Traditional skills are not as important as they once were, but they still have some value for the cognitive benefits they cultivate. Examples of these skills are hand accounting, using the Dewey decimal system, doing long division, doing manual square roots, and writing by hand. There's nothing wrong with these skills; they're just not as important as they once were, because the tasks to which they apply can now be accomplished more easily with new technologies.

Handwriting, for example, is a great skill for students to learn in primary school for the cognitive development it promotes, and it's still a great skill today for personal note-taking, but when was the last time you composed a handwritten letter and mailed it? How many businesspeople send handwritten letters to customers? It's a nice touch, but in general, handwriting is an example of something that simply isn't as important as it once was.

Insisting that our students continue to develop their handwriting skills to complete an essay or report is a classic example of an Industrial Age mindset being focused on a diminished Industrial Age skill. Do you remember when students used to pass handwritten notes? Have new technologies replaced that skill?

Traditional Literacy Skills

This set of skills remains as valuable today as it ever was. These skills include the traditional literacies—skills such as reading, writing, numeracy, research skills, communications skills, and traditional face-to-face social skills and the like.

The reason that these skills continue to be so important is because they are essential to interpersonal communication. These traditional skills are as important today as they were in the past.

Traditional Skills With Increased or Differentiated Emphasis

Traditional skills with increased or differentiated emphasis are skills that have recently received a promotion. Because of the emergence of the information media age, these skills have had more emphasis placed on them in the 21st century. They include information processing, critical thinking, problem solving, an understanding of how to use various new technologies, understanding the principles of graphic design, video and sound production, photo editing, and imaginative storytelling.

These are not new skills, but there is an increasing emphasis placed on them because of the emergence of digital culture. For example, in the Industrial Age, critical thinking and information processing were done primarily by management, which formed only a small percentage of the workforce.

Today, frontline workers must routinely search online information services, critically process retrieved information, and make decisions in order to perform daily business tasks. Unlike in the Industrial Age, when only university-bound students needed these skills, in our time, the vast majority of students, not just an academic elite, need 21st-century fluency skills if they are to succeed in the world that awaits them once they leave school.

Skills Unique to the 21st Century

These are the skills that weren't necessary 10 or 15 years ago. Many of them have been created by the emergence of new digital technologies. These skills include competence with social networking, online communications, digital citizenship, and 21st-century collaboration. This is a rapidly growing and constantly changing set of skills. As new technologies are created and adopted, these skills morph to accommodate them.

The Long and the Short of It

Ask yourself this question: In your classroom and in your school, is your focus on short- or long-term goals?

When we ask this question to teachers and administrators, the most frequent answer is that the focus is a well-balanced blend of both short- and long-term goals. Perhaps it's the answer you gave, but let's think about this for a moment.

We focus on getting our students ready for the next day, the next topic, the next test, the next term, the next level of education. We use the test data from the previous year to drive our instructional decisions and learning strategies for the coming year. We look at the data to figure out how we can get students next year to perform better on the same tests. Are we really focused on the long term?

This may seem like a blend of long-term and short-term planning, but really it's just a series of short-term plans. Education cannot be just about repeated short-term goals. Its true purpose is not just about getting students ready for the next day or the next topic, term, bubble test, or level. Education has to be about identifying the skills, knowledge, and habits of mind that all of our students will need to be successful in their life beyond school.

Ironically enough, we are already more than a decade into the 21st century but are still debating what 21st-century skills are and what 21st-century teaching should look like. Yet an interesting global consistency exists. We consult with stakeholders at many levels and in many countries, including parents, educators, administrators, businesspeople, and government officials, who all ask this same question: "What skills will students need most to succeed in the 21st century?"

Take a moment and ask yourself this same question. What is your answer? Next, ask this question to your colleagues. Ask it at your next staff meeting. Time and time again, we hear exactly the same answers. It doesn't matter what country we're in. It doesn't matter who the stakeholders are. Consistently, these are the answers we hear most:

Problem solving: Students need the ability to solve complex problems in real time.

Creativity: Students need to be able to think and creatively in both digital and nondigital environments to develop unique and useful solutions.

Analytic thinking: Students need the ability to think analytically, which includes facility with comparing, contrasting, evaluating, synthesizing, and applying without instruction or supervision and being able to use the higher end of Bloom's taxonomy.

Collaboration: Students must possess the ability to collaborate seamlessly in both physical and virtual spaces, with real and virtual partners globally.

Communication: Students must be able to communicate, not just with text or speech, but in multiple multimedia formats. They must be able to communicate visually, through video and imagery, in the absence of text, as actively as they do with text and speech.

Ethics, Action, Accountability: This cluster includes responses such as adaptability, fiscal responsibility, personal accountability, environmental awareness, empathy, tolerance, and many more. Though the language may vary a little, every group of stakeholders (parents through to national-level officials) give us more or less the same answers.

If we think about it for a moment, these are our long-term goals. If we are stating that by the end of their educational career, our students must have acquired these skills, then these would be true long-term educational goals we need to achieve. Now, ask yourself if your students are developing these skills. Are the skills in the mandated curriculum? Is there a system of accountability in place for you to evaluate and ensure that students are developing these critical skills? Or are we just hoping it happens along the way?

We are already more than a decade into the 21st century but are still debating what 21st-century skills are.

If we are honest with ourselves, we have to admit that our focus is almost exclusively on short-term goals. If we do not have a structured system for ensuring our students develop 21st-century skills, then there is simply no way to help them develop them. The skills they'll need to succeed in the world beyond school are the priority; they're not optional.

Teaching 21st-Century Fluencies as Processes

By now, we are sure that you share with us the understanding of the pressing need to cultivate 21st-century fluencies in every student. When we first started discussing how to do this and how to assist educators in making it happen, we quickly realized that we needed a process or system that educators could use with their students.

It's easy for us to say, "Kids need problem-solving skills." But this begs these questions: "What do these skills look like? What do they look like in the real world? What do they look like in my classroom? How do I teach them? How do students learn them? How can I assess them?"

We had the same questions. Over the next few chapters, we will share with you the 21st-century fluencies—structured processes for the skills we defined earlier. These processes can be taught, they can be learned, and they can be internalized by your students.

These aren't just for the students, though. The 21st-century fluencies are process skills that we all need, and there is as much benefit in cultivating them within yourself as within your classroom.

Summarizing the Main Points

- We need to move our thinking and our training beyond our primary focus and fixation on the Three Rs to a focus on skills that foster critical thinking, creativity, and problem-solving skills.

- There are five skill categories: obsolete skills, traditional skills, traditional literacy skills, traditional skills with increased or differentiated emphasis, and skills unique to the 21st century.

- Unlike in the Industrial Age, when only university-bound students needed these skills, in our time, the vast majority of students, not just an academic elite, need 21st-century fluency skills if they are to succeed in the world that awaits them once they leave school.

- Education cannot be just about repeated short-term goals. Education has to be about identifying the skills, knowledge, and habits of mind that all of our students will need to be successful in their life beyond school.

- Our long-term education goals for the 21st-century learner are: problem solving, creativity, analytic thinking, collaboration, communication, and ethics, action, and accountability.

- The 21st-century fluencies are process skills that we all need, and there is as much benefit in cultivating them within yourself as within your classroom.

Questions to Consider

- What additional skills can you think of, above and beyond those mentioned in this chapter, that students will need to succeed in the 21st century?

- How do current methods of learning and thinking prohibit long-term educational goals?

- What could be the benefits in cultivating the 21st-century fluencies within yourself?

define   discover   dream   design   deliver   debrief

Chapter 4
Solution Fluency

> **Problems are only opportunities in work clothes.**
>
> Henry Kaiser

Literally dozens of books have been written about the effects of technology on business today: Thomas Friedman's *The World Is Flat,* Daniel Pink's *A Whole New Mind,* Jeremy Rifkin's *The Future of Work,* Donald Tapscott's *Wikinomics,* and our book, *Living on the Future Edge,* just to name a few.

These books point out that instant, global communication is a reality and that anything that can be outsourced has been or soon will be. In chapter 1, we talked about the evolution of the workforce and how technology is facilitating the outsourcing or automating of any job that involves only routine cognitive tasks.

Here is a global example: When you go through a drive-thru, there is a good chance the order was taken by someone in Taiwan or China and then relayed back to the point of sale system at the restaurant. The system takes your photograph to match it to the order when you get to the window.

Similarly, you know that requests for technical support, calls to report credit card billing problems, and inquiries about the results of patients' MRI scans are all received and addressed by people on the other side of the planet. Where does that leave us?

What we are left with are jobs that require whole-brain thinking, career opportunities that require the ability to think creatively, solve problems, and apply those solutions in real time. This is in alignment with the list of long-term goals we discussed in chapter 3.

How we teach problem solving in classrooms today isn't really working for us. Presenting a problem, then giving students the answer by showing them how we got it, and then repeating the process over and over by giving them a series of similar problems to solve doesn't cut it. When we do this, we aren't teaching them anything other than how smart we are. We are cultivating dependency, not independent thought and the ability to analyze and solve problems.

When we ask the question "What are the skills students will need most to succeed in the 21st century?" the most common answer given is that the students must be exceptional problem solvers.

In a 21st-century learning environment, the method is different. We provide problems that are interesting and relevant to students, problems whose solutions involve elements of the mandated curriculum. To guide the students, we provide them with the 6 Ds, a process by which they can solve any problem they encounter, and Solution Fluency, the ability to use the 6 Ds in an unconscious manner.

Let's give problem-solving skills a promotion and place them at the focal point of learning! Our unit plans are built on Solution Fluency. Each stage is a learning progression in which students receive formative feedback to guide them through the process.

The Process

Define

It all starts with defining the problem. Yogi Berra said, "If you don't know where you're going, you'll end up someplace else." To define a problem is to identify it and plan where we're going with it before we start. It sounds obvious, but so often we don't define a problem, or at least we don't define it completely. In 21st-century fluency unit plans, the first learning progression is a written definition of the problem, because it is critical that we take the time to distinguish a clear problem-solving approach and avoid the classic ready, fire, aim—or ready, aim, backfire—problem-solving approach used by many people today.

Define skills include restating, or rephrasing the problem; challenging assumptions; gathering facts; chunking the details up or down (pulling them together or breaking them down into smaller parts); considering the challenge from multiple perspectives; and reversing the problem.

Discover

With a clear understanding of the problem, we can stand in the present, look to the past, and consider how we got into this mess. Discover is our exploration phase. How did we get to this point? What decisions were made in the past that brought us here? What could have been done differently that would have produced a different result? Does that still apply? How have others before us looked at this problem? What has worked under similar circumstances?

The reason we are asking these questions, and the whole purpose of Discover, is that it gives us a context in which to better understand the problem. We move beyond the intellectual definition and gain a solid grasp of the issues behind the problem. Perhaps we can even gain an emotional connection or inspire some passion about creating a solution.

Discover skills include determining where the information is; skimming, scanning, and scouring the information for background; filtering; taking smart notes; analyzing, authenticating, and arranging the materials; and knowing when to revisit the Define (or Discover, Dream, or Design) stage to modify what has been done based on what has been discovered.

Dream

With our clear understanding of where we are (Define) and how we got here (Discover), and with our passion to solve the problem ignited, we are armed with everything we need to turn to the future and dream a solution. Dream is a whole-mind process, one that allows us to imagine the solution as it will exist in the future. This is a visioning process in which we not only imagine what is possible but also remain open to what is impossible.

Conceptualize what might be. Open your mind and ask, "Why not?" It is through unlimited visioning—a skill in high demand but short supply—that innovation occurs. We will talk about the Dream phase in more detail when we discuss Creativity Fluency. For now, let's consider that we have our solution and it's time to move to the Design phase.

Dream skills include generating wishes, exploring possibilities, imagining best case scenarios, and visualizing time machine visits to a perfect future.

Design

Define tells us where we are now. Dream helps us decide where we want to go. Design becomes the process of gap analysis, breaking out all the necessary steps to get us from here to there. It's been said that "a carelessly planned project will take three times longer than the time allotted, but a very carefully planned project will only take twice as long." Have you ever heard this statement? There's a lot of truth in it. We must create a plan to guide us as we work. A plan is our blueprint or roadmap, a logical strategy that keeps us on track and helps avoid wasted effort. A plan can be checked, discussed, and re-evaluated. In Design, we build backward from the future, identifying the milestones and creating achievable deadlines.

Design skills include having a clear idea of how to do the task, starting with the end in mind and building steps backwards, and writing instructions in small increments that are easy to follow, positive and logical

Deliver

Putting the plan into action and making the dream a reality is delivering the solution. There are two components to Deliver: Produce and Publish. In the 21st-century classroom, students create a real-world product or solution. The product can be almost anything. The students may perform a play, build a sculpture, produce a video, complete an experiment, create a web site, or make a multimedia presentation. The possibilities are endless.

But producing is only half the work. They have to go all the way and deliver (publish) the solution. Designing a presentation isn't enough; it has to be presented. Writing a song isn't enough; it has to be recorded. Developing a script isn't enough; the work has to be performed. Students must deliver the goods. There is a good reason for this. Without fully implementing their solution, they will never know if it will work.

Seeing the product delivered allows for valuable information and feedback. You can't simply create a hypothesis and not run the experiment. Without the action and the results, it remains only a hypothesis.

Deliver skills include being able to identify the most appropriate format for presenting the information and using that format to present the information or solution to the problem.

Debrief

In the world outside of school, the responsibility for one's work and the ramifications of it continue long after production of an initial product. However, in a traditional school setting, teachers do most of the evaluation in the classroom. Students get the idea that work is a linear process—it begins with an assignment and ends when they hand something in. They receive a letter or numeral for a grade, with indications of what they did incorrectly.

However, in a 21st-century classroom, students are involved in the evaluation process through both self- and peer assessment. It is through these assessments that they develop ownership of the solution and a sense of accountability. Debrief offers students the opportunity to look at the final product and the process to determine what was done well and what could have been done better. In our experience, once students have been involved in the debrief phase, they start to pre-debrief by themselves and make improvements to their products before they present them. Debrief skills include being able to re-visit each stage of the process and reflect upon the pathways that were followed to get from Define to Deliver; asking questions about the processes used and information obtained; reflecting critically on both the process and the product, acting on those reflections, and internalizing the new learnings; and transferring the learning to new and different circumstances..

Solution Fluency is not a linear process but a cyclical one. At any point in the process, students may be led to retrace their steps. Sometimes in the Deliver phase, a new idea appears that leads a student back to Design. Or perhaps in Discover, the student realizes that the definition really wasn't clear and must be revised.

A thorough understanding of Solution Fluency and experience with it will help your students navigate through complex problems within the classroom and in their personal lives. In the future, when life throws them a curve, instead of being paralyzed in a personal crisis, they will know to stop, take a deep breath, and say, "Okay, the first thing I have to do is define the problem."

Make the shift to a 21st-century learning environment. Take the 6 Ds of solution fluency—define, discover, dream, design, deliver, and debrief—and put them on the wall of your classroom. Provide your students with interesting, relevant problems and guide them through the process of solving them using Solution Fluency. Empower them with the problem-solving skills that are so critical to their future.

She Blinded Me With Science

The 6 Ds echo work on *Appreciative Inquiry* by David Cooperrider of Case Western Reserve University (http://en.wikipedia.org/wiki/Appreciative_inquiry), Ted McCain in *Teaching for Tomorrow,* and many others.

There exist several systems of problem-solving techniques. In developing Solution Fluency, we wanted to create a comprehensive approach that could be easily taught to students. We came up with a system they could remember and apply—a cyclical and all-encompassing process that could be used in any application. We found our inspiration in a system we all learned in the high school chemistry lab.

The 6 Ds can be applied not only in the scientific method but also in the writing process, media production, or just about any other field in which a solution needs to be developed and implemented.

Solution Fluency	Scientific Method	Writing Process	Media Production
Define	Aim	Prewriting	Preproduction
Discover	Background/ Introduction	Prewriting	Preproduction
Dream	Hypothesis	Prewriting	Preproduction
Design	Equipment/Method	Draft	Preproduction
Deliver (Produce)	Experiment	Revision/Editing	Production
Deliver (Publish)	Results	Publish	Postproduction
Debrief	Conclusion	Review	Review

A comparison of the Solution Fluency 6 Ds process to standard production formulas.

Solution Fluency in the Real World

David, a friend of ours, owns a restaurant that has been our local favorite for almost 30 years. During that time, many things have changed, both in the restaurant industry and in society. Staying successful in the restaurant business is often more difficult than becoming successful, and David has done a wonderful job of staying successful at it—primarily because he understands how to adapt to change. We'll examine some of the ways he has made changes.

The past decade has seen a significant shift in how businesses interact with their employees, and how those employees, in turn, interact with them. Loyalty, from both the company and the employee, is almost a thing of the past. People need a stronger reason than just their paycheck to remain in any one job for an extended period of time. This is especially true for workers in the restaurant industry, who tend to view their employment as a transitional step, not often as a career. It takes a great deal of time, energy, and money to effectively train an employee in any business, so keeping employees is of course cheaper and easier than replacing them. Retaining employees does, however, require attention and innovative action. The following is the story of how our friend developed a system for dealing with the challenges of employee retention in the restaurant industry.

Here Today, Gone Tomorrow (Define)

The first step was to clearly define the problem. When using the 6 Ds, it's important not to think too far ahead. It would be easy to be overwhelmed by thinking of all the reasons why there is a problem before it's been clearly defined. The problem in this case was quite simple:

We are having difficulty retaining employees for an extended period of time. Seasonal employees, such as those who return to school, often don't come back the following year. How can we keep our permanent, full-time employees and also have our seasonal employees return each year during the peak season? This is a simple and clear definition of the problem and the challenge.

Getting to the Heart of the Matter (Discover)

David looked at the problem and started asking himself the question, "Why do employees leave?" He thought perhaps it was money. Maybe throwing money at the problem would make it go away. He knew of a café owner in the same town who had increased his employees' salaries to almost three times the minimum wage—twice as much as any other café. But this owner found that money didn't make the difference. His employees still lacked a sense of commitment.

David asked other business owners who had put in place a profit-sharing system how effective this had been in retaining employees. The response was similar—there was a marginal increase in the length of time employees would stay, but still there was no sense of commitment or partnership. Throwing money at the problem, at least in the form of income, didn't seem to be the solution.

Then David decided the best way to find out why employees leave was to ask them! So he began the process of interviewing each member of his staff. He contacted old employees who had left to interview them as well. What he discovered was something that really should be of no surprise but that most employers would never consider: The reason employees left was not money, but the lack of a sense of purpose. Every one of us, and every one of them, needs to feel that we are accomplishing something. We all need to have something that is important to us, something we love or feel passionate about. Each of us wants to have the opportunity to develop. The simple fact of the matter was, David found, that people were not fulfilled in their jobs. Pouring coffee or clearing tables was just something they were doing until they could do what they really wanted to do. As a result, people quickly became dissatisfied with their jobs and moved on, even if it was only to work at another restaurant.

I Can See Clearly Now (Dream)

Because he had been so open-minded during the Discover process, David was able to gain insight into what the real problem was. He was also able to be honest with himself about a solution. If he wanted to retain employees, he was going to have to strike a balance between his needs and their needs. His need was to have long-term committed employees, and he knew his restaurant would benefit from this. His employees needed to feel fulfilled in their jobs and in their lives.

David imagined a partnership in which, instead of increasing his employees' salaries, he would use the money and invest his time to help them achieve their goals.

I Love It When a Plan Comes Together (Design)

David knew that he had to start with his existing employees and then move on to each new applicant to make this process work. He would start by interviewing all of his existing employees to find out what their dreams were and to find ways in which he could partner with them to help them realize those dreams. He would also explain what it was he was trying to accomplish and his reasons for wanting to start this program.

With each new hire, David went through a similar process. Over time, he began to discover what inspired his employees and tried to help them make their dreams a reality. For new hires, knowing what inspired them and how he could help was just as important as their qualifications.

Walking the Walk (Deliver)

As David began the process, he was surprised to find out exactly what it was that inspired people. While interviewing one employee, he found out that her greatest desire was to write and produce her own one-woman show. David happens also to be an accomplished filmmaker and producer, so together, they made a plan for her to work one day each week on her script rather than at the restaurant. Over the next several months, she wrote, produced, and performed her show. Three years later, she still works at the restaurant, and one day each week, she works on producing new shows.

Another employee, who was seasonal, was studying commerce at the university. Each summer, David's restaurant sponsors a film festival. It is a major event, and it takes a great deal of organization and management to make it happen successfully. David made an agreement to have this student take over the management duties for the festival. The employee then split his time between the restaurant and the festival.

One of David's older employees felt a strong need to work with the homeless, so David helped her set up program that allowed extra food from the restaurant to be taken to the local soup kitchen. She became the coordinator for the efforts of the restaurant to assist with this and other local charities. One day a week, her job is to manage these programs.

Looking Forward, Looking Back (Debrief)

Throughout the process, David met with his employees to monitor the success of their individual programs and make adjustments where necessary. This constant debriefing allowed him to keep everything on track, to see what was effective, and to see what wasn't effective. This helped him to consider what was possible with each new employee.

Three years later, all these employees still work for David. Many of the seasonal employees, such as the young man who managed the film festival, return each year. They require no training and are able to drop into their old jobs. Some of them also return during Christmas or spring break to visit their families and pick up a few shifts.

Analyzing the process, David found that when this program did not work for an employee, it was often because he had not been thorough in discovering what the true passion of the employee was, or else he had failed to monitor the employee's progress and provide enough support. David has adjusted his process accordingly, and in this constant cycle of fine-tuning, he has improved his results dramatically.

All in all, the program has been very successful. David is actually working on a book to help other business owners connect with their employees.

Solution Fluency Snapshot

To help you evaluate the level of proficiency that you or your students have with Solution Fluency, use this tool. You can use it with individual students or with groups.

There are 10 statements below for you to consider. As you move through the statements, chose a value you feel represents the how well the individual or group you are evaluating has demonstrated the characteristic. Rate each statement from 1 (*strongly disagree*) to 5 (*strongly agree*). Better still, have your students assess themselves and discuss the outcome.

Move down the list, and then add up your total and multiply it by 2. This is the student's Solution Fluency percentage, which you record in the box provided at the end of each list. From there, you can compare your results in each fluency to determine where focus and improvement may be needed.

solution fluency

Define
Discover
Dream
Design
Deliver
Debrief

	1	2	3	4	5
Clearly and accurately defines the problem to be addressed.					
Appropriately synthesizes information about the development of the problem.					
Consistently envisions a range of creative solutions to real-world problems.					
Considers many possible solutions before selecting the most appropriate and achievable one.					
Develops a complete step-by-step plan for solving the problem.					
Maintains a focus on the goals driving the problem-solving process.					
Revisits, reflects critically on, and revises the process at each stage.					
Uses wide range of media to communicate understanding of both content and process.					
Reflects critically on how the product and process can be improved once a solution has been developed.					
Demonstrates adaptability and commitment by modifying the product and process when weaknesses in either are identified.					

Solution Fluency   %

solution
fluency

Solution Fluency
Lesson Plan Grading Tool

The Lesson Plan Grading Tools are used to determine the degree of application of each of the 21st-century fluencies within the context of a unit plan. The Fluency Matrix is located on the front page of every unit plan. It is represented by a vertical line of colorful fluency icons that represent each of the 21st-century fluencies.

Below are a series of statements for you to consider that help to define the characteristics of Solution Fluency within the context of a unit. Beside each statement is a 1 to 5 scale similar to the ones found in the Fluency Snapshot. As you work through each statement, consider the extent of its application in the unit, and rate each statement from 1 (*strongly disagree*) to 5 (*strongly agree*).

Move down the list, and then add your total up and multiply it by 2. This is the Solution Fluency percentage, which is an estimation of how effectively a unit plan focuses on it's development in your students.

Define
Discover
Dream
Design
Deliver
Debrief

1 2 3 4 5

The unit plan presents a clear problem/challenge to the students.

The problem/challenge has a real-world context.

The problem/challenge is engaging and relevant to students.

The challenge requires every student to create his or her own unique and effective solution.

The lesson plan guides students toward creative thought, critical thinking, and decision making when considering multiple solution possibilities.

The problem/challenge requires creation of a product as part of the problem-solving process.

The problem/challenge requires research and discovery of unrevealed knowledge.

The challenge encourages creation of a S.M.A.R.T solution—*specific, measurable, attainable, realistic*, and *timely.*

The solution is versatile, can be applied effectively to the context of the problem, and can be transferred for use in similar or different real-world situations.

The solution encourages critical reflection of both the product created and process undertaken.

%   Solution Fluency

Summarizing the Main Points

- How we teach problem solving in classrooms today isn't really working. We are cultivating dependency, not independent thought and the ability to analyze and solve problems.

- In a 21st-century learning environment, we provide problems that are interesting and relevant to students, problems whose solutions involve elements of the mandated curriculum.

- To guide the students, we provide them with the 6 Ds (Define, Discover, Dream, Design, Deliver, and Debrief).

- Solution Fluency is the ability to use the 6 Ds in an unconscious manner.

- Solution Fluency is not a linear process but a cyclical one.

Questions to Consider

- Are you unconsciously already using some of the 6 Ds? Are there certain ones you never really use?

- What challenge or problem could you apply the 6 Ds to in your life right now?

- Could Dave's idea of connecting with his employees also work in a classroom environment between teachers and students?

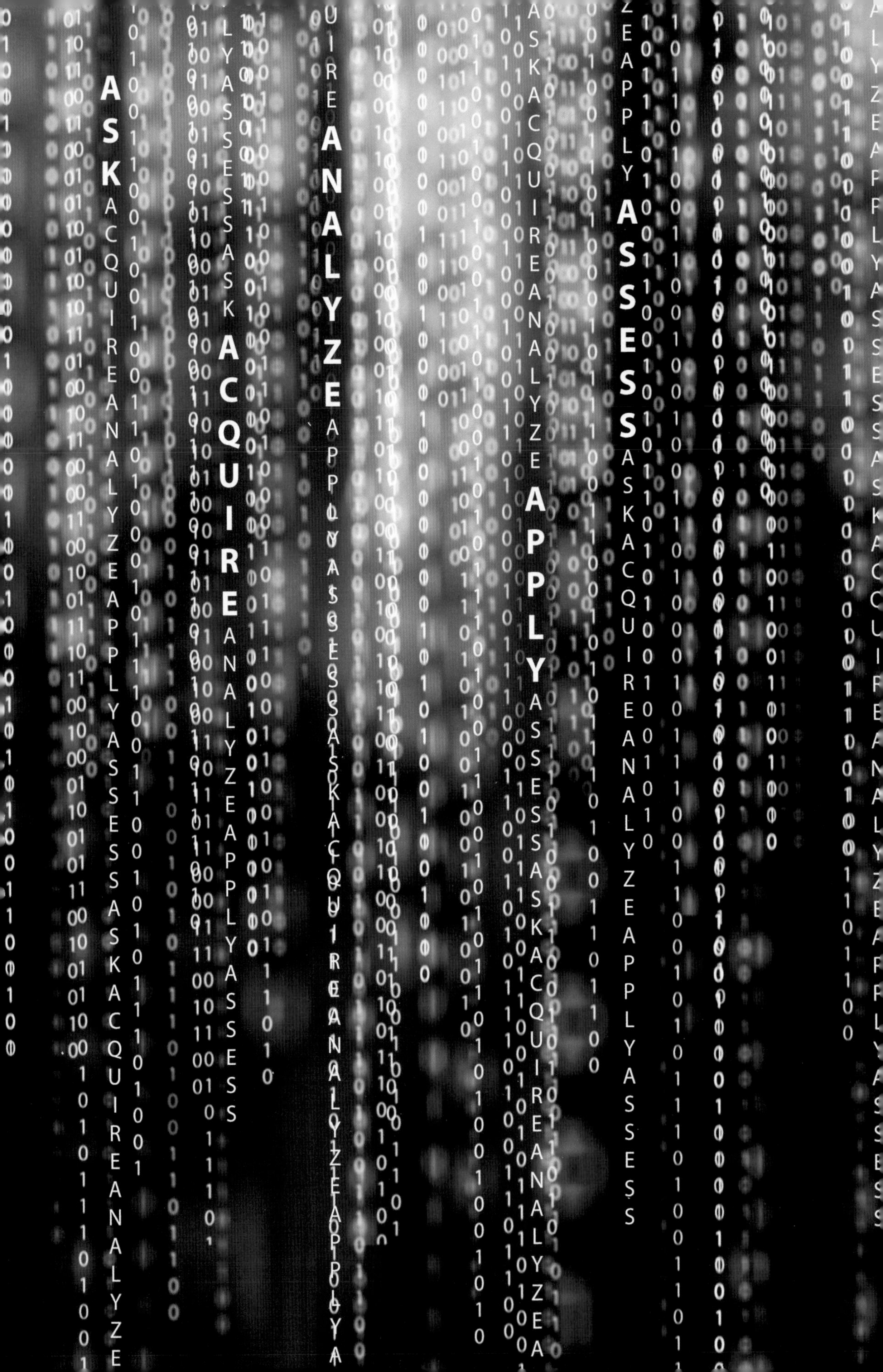
ASK
ACQUIRE
ANALYZE
APPLY
ASSESS

Chapter 5
Information Fluency

> **The most serious mistakes are not being made as a result of wrong answers. The truly dangerous thing is asking the wrong questions.**
>
> Peter Drucker, *Men, Ideas & Politics*

As we wrote in our recent book, *Living on the Future Edge*, we live in an age of InfoWhelm. The unprecedented acceleration of the development of new technology in the last decades of the 20th century has precipitated a parallel change in the knowledge base. We live in a world awash in readily available information. As a result, facts become obsolete more quickly, and knowledge built on those facts becomes less durable. This has forced us to reorganize our knowledge and how we deliver it, and it is fundamentally altering the very fabric of our societies and irrevocably changing the way we work, play, communicate, and view our fellow citizens.

The Amount of Information in the World

According to the latest accounting of the world's information capacity, the tide of information we have unleashed is rising far faster than anyone expected. The flood of information is now a long-term tsunami.

Computing capacity is increasing at 58 percent annually, telecommunications at 28 percent, and storage at 23 percent per year. The former rate is approximately the rate of Moore's Law, a doubling every 18 months. Communications system capacities are doubling every 34 months, and storage every 40 months. Information has been expanding at this rate for the past decade.

These latest figures come from a February 2011 article, "The World's Technological Capacity to Store, Communicate, and Compute Information," by Martin Hilbert and Priscila Lopez.

The full scale of how much information we create is hard to appreciate. We humans collectively now have the capacity to store approximately 300 exabytes of information. This is close to the total amount of information stored in one person's DNA. Or, as Hilbert puts it, it's the equivalent of 80 Library of Alexandrias per person on the planet. And remember, the technium is doubling its capacity every year and a half, whereas your DNA is not.

As a result of InfoWhelm, we now live in an age of disposable information, one in which even the daily newspaper arrives out of date. Information has become a temporary and disposable commodity. Yes, information has value, but it is also just about as perishable as fruit. It may have a value today, but it will have to be discarded if it is not used by tomorrow.

With so much information available, no one today can be an expert. If our students are going to operate in an age of InfoWhelm, they need to be informationally fluent.

We define Information Fluency as the ability to unconsciously and intuitively interpret information in all forms and formats in order to extract the essential knowledge, perceive its meaning and significance, and use it to complete real-world tasks. There are five distinct steps to the Information Fluency process: Ask, Access, Analyze, Apply, and Assess.

"We live in the dynamic world of InfoWhelm, where content is growing exponentially in both quantity and complexity."

The Process

Ask

Ask good questions, because if you can't ask good questions, you won't get good answers. Critical asking skills include such things as understanding the problem to be solved, identifying key words, forming questions around key words, brainstorming, thinking laterally, understanding ethical issues, listening deeply, viewing wisely, speaking critically, filtering information white noise, and sharing personal knowledge and experience.

Acquire

It's only when students ask good questions that they will be able to access the raw materials from the most appropriate high-tech, low-tech, or no-tech sources. Acquire skills include determining where the information is; determining what skills are needed to find the information; prioritizing search strategies; skimming, scanning, and scouring the resources for pertinent data; filtering; taking smart notes; and knowing when it's necessary to go back to the initial Ask stage to ask more questions. In the digital landscape, accessing has become less and less about going to a card catalog and getting a book or other paper-based resources. More and more, students' most utilized search tools are YouTube, Twitter, blogs, Wikipedia, and music and interactive web sites. These digital resources increasingly provide the raw materials of the 21st century, and much of this material is graphic and audiovisual in nature. It's no longer just about the traditional book-based resources of our youth.

Analyze

With the raw data in hand, the next step is to analyze, authenticate, and arrange the materials. One of the scary things about the Internet is that it's an open sewer of untreated, unfiltered information. If students don't know how to navigate—if they can't determine whether something is really true or not—they'll just grab on to the first thing they find.

The Analyze and Authenticate skills include such things as organizing, triangulating, and summarizing data from a variety of sources. They involve working independently and collaboratively with peers, teachers, or other individuals to document the authenticity and analysis of the data and checking data for relevance and listing and distinguishing between good, bad, and ugly data sources. It's about being able to differentiate fact from opinion and assessing currency and examining data for underlying meaning and bias. With these skills, you must also be able to determine when the data answer the original questions and identify when there is incomplete information. For example, how many of you have ever bought a house or a car or married someone, based on incomplete information?

Finally, it involves documenting, crediting, and taking notes to determine authenticity, using probability, trends, and best guesses to seek out additional data as needed. It involves knowing when it's necessary to revisit the Ask or Access stage to fill in the blanks so that you can turn data into knowledge and wisdom.

Apply

Next, users must be able to apply that knowledge within the context of a real-life, real-world problem or a simulation of one. This skill, which we referred to as the Deliver or Do stage in the 6 Ds, involves putting the pieces together so that they can be used. It may involve writing an essay, developing a report, creating a graph, completing an argument, making a presentation, participating in a debate, completing a science experiment, creating a video, or building a blog. Apply is the stage in which products are created, actions taken, problems solved, and information needs satisfied. Being able to access huge amounts of data means nothing unless the data are effectively analyzed, turned into personal knowledge, and then applied to solving the problem.

Assess

After the product has been created, students must be able to assess both the product itself and the process. This is what we called Debrief in the 6 Ds of Solution Fluency.

Crucial assessing skills include being able to ask questions about the processes used and the information obtained; reflecting critically on the process; assessing what was learned, how it was learned, what worked, what didn't work, and how the process and the product could be made better the next time around; and then acting on these reflections, internalizing new learnings, and transferring them to other similar or different situations and circumstances.

We passionately believe that the 5 As of the Information Fluency process are the basis for meeting virtually any information need, and, as such, they must be considered to be as important as the 6 Ds—embedded into every lesson, every activity, and every task we ask our students to undertake.

Myth-information in the Real World

The DHMO Organization and its web site DHMO.org were created in late 1997 by Dr. Tom Way, a research scientist in Newark, Delaware. DHMO stands for dihydrogen monoxide. According to this site, DHMO has a strong link to cancer and environmental pollution, among many other things. The substance is the major component of acid rain and contributes to the "greenhouse effect." It may cause severe burns and is fatal if inhaled. It contributes to the erosion of our natural landscape, accelerates corrosion and rusting of many metals, and may cause electrical failures and decreased effectiveness of automobile brakes. It has also been found in excised tumors of terminal cancer patients.

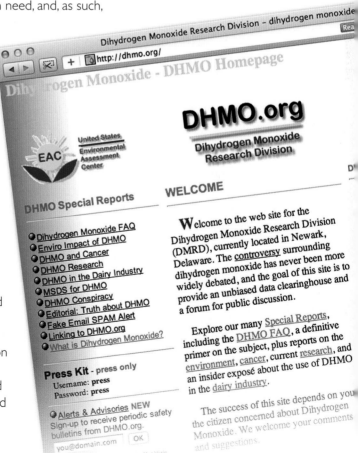

Despite the evident danger, DHMO is often used as an industrial solvent and coolant in nuclear power plants, in the production of Styrofoam, as a fire retardant, in many forms of cruel animal research, as an additive in certain "junk foods" and other food products, and in the distribution of pesticides. Even after washing, the product remains contaminated by this chemical.

We ask students to use the 5 As of Information Fluency to assess the risks of DHMO to humans and the environment. When they have finished this process, we debrief them on what happened. Some students will be absolutely outraged that such a chemical is so widely used. But if the students have faithfully followed the 5 As process, most will discover that DHMO is just an unfamiliar name for water. However, many students jump quickly through the steps in the process, ignoring critical elements.

By way of background, DHMO.org was originally created by three students from the University of California, Santa Cruz, in 1990. The site was brought to widespread public attention in 1997 when Nathan Zohner, a 14-year-old student, gathered petitions to ban "DHMO" as the basis of his science project, titled "How Gullible Are We?"

In 2001, a staff member in New Zealand Green Party Member of Parliament Sue Kedgley's office responded to a request by saying she was "absolutely supportive of the campaign to ban this toxic substance." This was criticized in press releases by the opposition National Party, one of whose members, Jacquie Dean, fell for the very same hoax six years later, when she wrote to the National Health Associate Minister asking if DHMO should be banned.

Information Fluency in the Real World

Karen and her two teenage daughters, Lisa and Shona, decided they could finally afford to take the plunge and buy their first cell phones. But at first glance, they were absolutely shocked to discover how many brands and types of cell phones there were, each with a wide range of features. Then, there was the confusing array of service plans that the different companies offered. To ensure that they would make an informed decision, they decided to create a chart illustrating the strengths and weaknesses of the services provided by the various cell phone carriers and the cell phones that best met their needs. This is the story of how they came to their big decision.

Ask

Most of their friends had bought either the first cell phone they looked at or the one that was most popular at the time. Karen had recently heard a news report that consumers worldwide were wasting hundreds of dollars on cell phone and data packages each year because they had not researched their needs and the plans available.

Karen and her daughters were determined to make an informed decision rather than an impulsive one. The first thing they had to do was identify the questions they needed answered to help them make the right choice. They formulated the questions through brainstorming and identifying key words:

- What plans do the various carriers offer (e.g., prepaid, fixed-term contract, pay-as-you-go, locked/unlocked, or family plan)?

- What services do the various carriers offer (phone, text, email, data, image, media, apps, gaming)?

- What features do they need in their cell phone plan, and which ones will they use most often (voice quality, messaging, camera, media playback, keyboard, Web, GPS, gaming)?

- What are the pricing plans?

Acquire

Next, they identified the five most popular national carriers and accessed the information that would answer their questions. They visited the web sites and the storefronts of AT&T, Sprint, U.S. Cellular, and Verizon to download and gather as much background information as possible. There was an enormous amount of information about plans, services, and cell phones available.

While wading through the details, they realized that they had forgotten to include Internet phones and low-cost services such as Cricket in their search. That caused them to go back and adjust their questions to include additional possibilities.

Analyze

Then, they sat down and started to organize and analyze all the information they had acquired. They created lists that summarized the data and read as many reviews as possible to learn the expert opinions on the best smartphones, cell phones, budget smartphones, budget cell phones, Internet phones, texting phones, and camera phones. They used this information to examine the many claims that the various companies made about their services and their phones. They quickly realized there was still more information that could be obtained from various other sources, such as the Readers' Choice Awards, *Consumer Reports*, and Amazon, so they went back to the Access stage to gather more information. They made sure to document, credit, and reference their original sources just in case they needed to revisit them at a later date.

Apply

With all the groundwork done, Karen and her daughters assembled the information they had gathered from the various sources. As they pulled all the information together and discussed the various features, it quickly became clear that what they needed and wanted was the three-year family plan that included new phones for each of them with unlimited, free local and incoming calls, 100 minutes of long distance, and 500 shared text messages a month. They decided not to purchase a data plan until they had a better handle on how much the plan would actually cost and whether it was practical for them. Finally, they needed to assess the process they had undertaken.

Assess

As they sat at their kitchen table playing with their new phones, they discussed how effective the process of identifying a plan and phone had been. Instead of the impulsive decision they made last year when they bought a new plasma TV—a decision they quickly regretted—they were very pleased to have taken the time to carefully map out, modify, and complete the decision-making process. It was a process that taught them some terrific skills they could apply to other situations in the future. Next on the list for them was a new car!

Information Fluency Snapshot

To help you evaluate the level of proficiency that you or your students have with Information Fluency, use this tool. You can use it with individual students or with groups.

There are 10 statements below for you to consider. As you move through the statements, chose a value you feel represents the how well the individual or group you are evaluating has demonstrated the characteristic. Rate each statement from 1 (*strongly disagree*) to 5 (*strongly agree*). Better still, have your students assess themselves and discuss the outcome.

Move down the list, and then add up your total and multiply it by 2. This is the student's Information Fluency percentage, which you record in the box provided at the end of each list. From there, you can compare your results in each fluency to determine where focus and improvement may be needed.

Ask
Acquire
Analyze
Apply
Assess

1 2 3 4 5

Defines information needs, identifies key words, and forms questions around them.

Determines most appropriate sources for collecting information.

Triangulates and gathers information from a broad range of media sources.

Demonstrates effective search, filtering, and note-taking strategies.

Uses effective strategies to analyze and authenticate information and make it useful.

Verifies accuracy of information obtained from various sources.

Separates fact from opinion, recognizes bias, and identifies incomplete information.

Cites and records all references accurately when gathering information.

Effectively applies knowledge within the originally required context.

Reflects critically on application of information and gathering process, making revisions for improvement.

_____ %   Information Fluency

Information Fluency
Lesson Plan Grading Tool

The Lesson Plan Grading Tools are used to determine the degree of application of each of the 21st-century fluencies within the context of a unit plan. The Fluency Matrix is located on the front page of every unit plan. It is represented by a vertical line of colorful fluency icons that represent each of the 21st-century fluencies.

Below are a series of statements for you to consider that help to define the characteristics of Information Fluency within the context of a unit. Beside each statement is a 1 to 5 scale similar to the ones found in the Fluency Snapshot. As you work through each statement, consider the extent of its application in the unit, and rate each statement from 1 (*strongly disagree*) to 5 (*strongly agree*).

Move down the list, and then add your total up and multiply it by 2. This is the Information Fluency percentage, which is an estimation of how effectively a unit plan focuses on it's development in your students.

information fluency

Ask
Acquire
Analyze
Apply
Assess

	1	2	3	4	5
The challenge requires a search for essential information that contributes to the overall solution.					
The challenge requires a search for information from various sources and media.					
The challenge requires a search for information using both digital and non-digital means.					
The challenge requires students to access, incorporate, and use information from multiple sources.					
The challenge encourages students to develop and utilize proper research techniques and strategies.					
The challenge requires students to critically analyze information to document its reliability, accuracy, and relevance.					
The challenge requires students to triangulate information by cross-verification from two or more sources.					
The challenge requires students to record/cite/acknowledge all sources of information accurately and correctly.					
The challenge requires students to organize information strategically into useful frameworks for reference and utilization.					
The challenge encourages critical reflection of both the product created and process undertaken.					

Information Fluency   %

Summarizing the Main Points

- According to the latest accounting of the world's information capacity, the tide of information we have unleashed is rising far faster than anyone expected.

- We now live in an age of disposable information, one in which even the daily newspaper arrives out of date. Information has become a temporary and disposable commodity.

- Information Fluency is the ability to unconsciously and intuitively interpret information in all forms and formats to extract the essential knowledge, perceive its meaning and significance, and use it to complete real-world tasks.

- There are five distinct steps to the Information Fluency process: Ask, Acquire, Analyze, Apply, and Assess.

Questions to Consider

- How would you define someone who is "informationally fluent"?

- Why is it increasingly important for today's students to be able to differentiate fact from opinion and examine data for underlying meaning and bias?

- Can you think of a time when you read or heard a piece of information that sounded wrong to you? How did you go about verifying it?

Chapter 6
Creativity Fluency

The MFA is the new MBA.

Daniel Pink

Most people believe that creativity is important for achieving success in the future and is thus an attribute that all students need to develop. But few people understand that teaching creativity is an absolute imperative and that we are falling behind the rest of the world in this area.

You are probably familiar with IQ tests, those standardized tools for measuring intelligence. But did you know that with IQ tests, there is a phenomenon called the Flynn Effect, named after New Zealand college professor Dr. James Flynn, which refers to the observation that every decade, IQ scores go up about 3 points (Neisser, 1997)? A simple explanation for this gain is that increasingly enriched environments are making kids smarter. For example, if the average score in 1932 was 100, by 2012 it would be approximately 124. The IQ scale has to be constantly adjusted to keep 100 as the median score.

Similarly, we can measure creativity, or the creative quotient (CQ), with the Torrance Tests of Creative Thinking (TTCT), developed by Dr. E. Paul Torrance. Like IQ tests, the Torrance tests have also shown the Flynn Effect, with scores around the world going up about 3.2 points every 10 years.

Recently, Kyung Hee Kim, an associate professor of educational psychology at the College of William & Mary in Williamsburg, Virginia, analyzed 300,000 Torrance scores of children and adults taken since the tests were first developed in 1966 (Britannica, 2010). The findings from her research illustrated that creativity scores, like IQ scores, had risen steadily until 1990. Since then, though, a reverse trend has been identified. Creativity scores since 1990 have been moving downward. It's clear that the decrease is significant, but more disturbing is the fact that it is accelerating. And for scores of younger children in America—those from kindergarten through sixth grade—the decline is most serious.

There is one crucial difference between IQ and CQ scores. IQ tests measure intelligence. The TTCT measures many different aspects of creativity, such as originality, abstractness, and open-mindedness. As Kim noted, "The TTCT measures the creative mind more broadly; it measures creative potential in many diverse areas such as art, literature, science, mathematics, architecture, engineering, business, leadership, and interpersonal relationships" (Britannica, 2010).

From 1984 to 1990, Elaboration scores on the TTCT (scores showing the ability to develop and elaborate on ideas, to engage in analytical thinking, and to be motivated to be creative) decreased by 19.41 percent. By 1998, they had decreased by 24.62 percent, and by 2008, the scores had plummeted 36.80 percent from the 1984 levels.

By the way, this decline in scores is primarily happening in the United States. Once a beacon to the world and a haven for those desiring the opportunity for creative expression, the United States is now falling behind the rest of the world.

It's too early to determine conclusively why U.S. creativity scores are declining. One possible culprit is the number of hours kids spend in front of the TV and playing video games rather than engaging in creative activities. Another might be the lack of creativity development in our

schools. With the focus on standards and high-stakes testing, many schools are guilty of scripting the learning environment to the point where spontaneity is viewed as counterproductive and disruptive. Abstractness, open-mindedness, and originality may be considered time thieves that steal time away from preparation for the high-stakes testing that dominates our current educational environment. As a consequence, there may be little, if any, concerted effort to nurture creativity at all.

While this is happening in America, many other countries are seizing the opportunity to invest in a culture of creativity by modeling what the United States used to be. All around us, matters of national and international importance are crying out for creative solutions— from global warming, to overpopulation, to combating terrorism and militancy, to saving the Gulf of Mexico, to bringing peace to Afghanistan, to delivering affordable health care, to shutting down out-of-control nuclear power plants to prevent a meltdown. All these endeavors require outside-the-box thinking. And these other countries, the ones that are cultivating creativity, will be poised to step in to offer solutions to these and other global issues.

Creativity is the currency of the 21st century. Creative individuals and nations are poised to prosper. The new Third World will be the nations that have to import creativity. Let's be clear. This isn't about some far-off murky future. It is already happening. As routine cognitive work and manufacturing jobs are outsourced, the only jobs left are likely to be creative-class jobs—the jobs that require higher-level thinking. Nonroutine cognitive work that can't be outsourced, replaced by software, or automated will be in high demand. Businesses are turning to creativity like never before.

For example, do you know the image on the left? You probably recognize it as a hotel in Dubai. It is the Burj Al Arab, and it has become as synonymous with Dubai as the Sydney Opera House is to Australia or the Eiffel Tower to France. But think about the function of a hotel for a moment. Its basic purpose is to provide accommodations—a bed and a shower. Everything else is a perk. With this in mind, we have to ask, why does the Burj Al Arab hotel look like this? It doesn't have to. It could be just a boxlike structure with rooms for guests, which would certainly be functional. However, it wouldn't have the same appeal, would it?

They wouldn't be able to charge their hugely expensive rates if it was just a box. Rooms in this hotel are as much as $28,000 per night, and you have to pay more than $50 just to walk in and look at the lobby. Of course, the luxurious accommodations and service keep it running, but luxury and outstanding service don't always come with a $28,000 price tag. There's something more than just the function of the building going on here. Its real value comes from its unique and recognizable shape. Its form sets it apart from any other hotel in the world and makes it a desirable destination. This valuing of form is being echoed throughout the business world.

Changing Values in the Marketplace

A few years ago, General Motors hired a new executive, Robert Lutz, to help turn the company around. Because Lutz was a former Marine and a seasoned businessman, you would expect his approach to be regimented and no-nonsense. When asked by the *New York Times* how his approach would be different than that of his predecessors, he said:

> *"It's more right-brained. . . . I see us in the art business. Art, entertainment, and mobile sculpture that coincidentally happens to provide transportation."*

As another example, take this statement made by Norio Ohga, the former chairman of Sony Corporation, as quoted in *Re-Imagine* magazine in 2003:

> *"At Sony, we assume that all products of our competitors have basically the same technology, price, performance, and features. Design is the only thing that differentiates one product from another in the marketplace."*

These startling statements highlight a remarkable shift away from the traditional 20th-century focus on the left-brain thinking that focused on the features and performance of a product. According to Paul Thompson, the director of the Cooper-Hewitt Museum in New York:

> *"Manufacturers have begun to recognize that we can't compete with the pricing structure and labor costs of the Far East. So how can we compete? It has to be with design."*

Norman Podhoretz puts it this way:

> *"Creativity represents a miraculous coming together of the uninhibited energy of the child with its apparent opposite and enemy, the sense of order imposed on the disciplined adult intelligence."*

In his book *A Whole New Mind*, Daniel Pink (2006) says that the wealth of nations and the well-being of individuals now depends on having artists in the room when anything is created. Imagine that—having artists involved in creative ventures. It sounds a bit like common sense, doesn't it?

Pink tells the story of a professor who went into a kindergarten class one day and asked students to raise their hands if they could dance. Their hands all shot into the air. He asked how many could dance or sing, and again, they all raised their hands. Then, he went into a college class and asked the same questions of students there, and of course, no one raised their hands. He concluded that education is the process of teaching us what we can't do.

But school shouldn't take all the blame. We also do this to ourselves. Lee recounts a realization he had while in art school in Florence, Italy. Every day, he and the other students would study the human form by drawing live models. It's tough to do, as there isn't a straight line on the human body, and this exercise is an excellent and time-honored way of cultivating talent and an appreciation for beauty.

One particular day, Lee had his charcoal in one hand and a rubber eraser in the other. It wasn't a good day, and the hand with the eraser was doing most of the work. As his frustration grew, Lee heard a voice telling him how bad his work was, how it wasn't as good as the other students', and how it didn't look anything like the model.

Lee took a break and went for a walk. Around the corner from the art school is a special church, Santa Croce, in which both Galileo and Michelangelo are buried. As Lee sat in front of Michelangelo's tomb contemplating the day, he had a realization: the voices that were criticizing his work were his own. More important, he realized that his dissatisfaction was with his technical delivery, and that this is not the same as creativity.

> *We all are creative. It's not our creativity that's in question, it's our technical proficiency.*

Scott Adams, the renowned creator of the *Dilbert* comic strip, wrote this in his iconic book, *The Dilbert Principle*:

> *"Creativity is allowing yourself to make mistakes. Art is knowing which ones to keep."*

During our developmental process, we unconsciously start comparing ourselves and our work to others. Our internal critic tells us we aren't good enough. We convince ourselves that we are not talented and that we are not creative. But we all are creative. It's not our creativity that's in question, it's our technical proficiency. If you missed out on fingerpainting, we urge you to try it. Break out the fingerpaints at your next staff meeting.

What Lee realized is that we confuse these two concepts. As a result, we believe that we are not creative. We've all heard people say that they don't have a creative bone in their body. What they really should be saying is that they are lacking in the technical aspects of delivering their ideas. Be assured that you can create and you are creative—we all are. Technical proficiency comes with practice. When Lee left art school, his technical ability was an order of magnitude above where it had been when he started drawing the human form for hours each day as a warm-up.

And just as technical proficiency can be taught, so can the creative process. It is just that—a process, which can be taught and learned. It's a whole-brain process that involves both hemispheres working together using the 5 Is of Creativity Fluency.

The Process

Identify

The first I in the creative process is Identify. You begin by preloading your brain with the data of the current problem. Start by asking yourself what your task is and what you need to create. Think back to Solution Fluency for a moment: your understanding of the problem comes from the Define stage, a step that adds context through Discovery. The synthesis of these two stages brings meaning and relevance to the problem. It makes it real.

The skills for Identify include understanding the problem to be solved; identifying key words and forming questions around them; brainstorming; thinking laterally; understanding ethical issues; listening deeply, viewing wisely, and speaking critically; filtering information white noise; and sharing personal knowledge and experience.

Inspire

When the left brain is primed with data, we are ready to begin the adventure by seeking inspiration. This is great fun, and it involves feeding your creative appetite with rich sensory information. This is the true Dream phase.

Inspiration can come from anywhere: scanning remote memories, visualizing, flipping through magazines, going to a museum, looking at color photo books or web sites, walking down the street, brainstorming over coffee, wandering around a bookstore, or listening to music that has a mood similar to what the outcome might look like.

Inspire skills would include being able to move beyond what is known, using familiar and unfamiliar sources to motivate and inspire, seeing new possibilities, playing with ideas, experimenting, and imagining.

You are looking to be inspired. Any of these actions may trigger an idea. However, all these activities are brain candy for the right hemisphere, which can be seduced into a black hole for a longer period of time than you might realize. This is why the left brain must keep vigil and keep us on track.

Interpolate

To interpolate means to find a pattern within known information. It is similar to finding a constellation in the sky by making a pattern appear from seemingly random information. When it does form, it's so obvious that it's all you can see, and you wonder how to you didn't see it before.

The left brain's job is to analyze the sensory inputs constantly arriving from your right brain playground of inspiration, trying to connect the dots by searching for patterns, alternate meanings, and high-level abstractions. Interpolation skills include pattern recognition, being able to identify connections or relationships, combining concepts or elements from different realms that would not normally be combined, and being able to think laterally about existing knowledge. Analyzing the sensory input means comparing it with the original criteria that you identify. You have to move past what doesn't match and hold on to the things that possibly do. Somewhere in all the random inputs is a connection, a solution waiting for you to imagine it.

Imagine

As you toggle back and forth in the process from Inspire to Interpolate, discarding extraneous information, you start to home in on a possible solution. There are little glimpses floating just outside your consciousness; you can sense them and almost see them! We've all had this experience, the "on-the-tip-of-my-tongue" moment, when the solution is just beyond your grasp. Continue searching, and the moment will come when the synthesis of Inspire and Interpolate unites in the birth of the idea that bursts from the periphery. Imagine is the "Aha!" moment.

Imagine skills include forming mental images, sensations, and concepts when they are not perceived through sight, hearing, or other senses; providing meaning to experience and understanding to make sense of the world through stories, art, music, poetry, video, and so forth.

Inspect

With our new creative idea imagined, we have to stand back and inspect. Does our idea meet the original criteria? Does it match our definition? Is it feasible? Will it work? Can it be accomplished within the existing time and budget?

Inspect skills include being able to examine the processes undertaken and the product created; being able to thoughtfully reflect on the process undertaken; visualizing the idea as if completed, comparing and contrasting it with the original purpose; and then using those reflections to internalize new ideas, revise the existing idea, and applying them to future challenges.

Sometimes the answer to these questions will be "no." Occasionally, the idea is a throwaway (but save it in case you can use it some other time). At other times, it may need adjustment, or it may lead to a new idea. This is why creativity fluency, much like all the 21st-century fluencies, is a cyclical process. You may need to move back to Inspire, or perhaps your idea points out flaws in your understanding of the problem and you will have to go back to Identify.

New Roles for the Arts Faculty

Creative fluency is the imaginative, artistic proficiency that has reached the unconscious ability to add meaning and value to things through design, art, and storytelling.

We think the role of the art teacher needs to be re-evaluated. Other faculty would be wise not to view the art teacher as the hippie down the hall and not to view art class as a waste of time. The art teacher should be considered the art director and should operate as a creative consultant to all other faculty.

It's not only art that is required in every classroom in a 21st-century learning environment. Consider the role of music in the production of a movie. The soundtrack carries much of the meaning. It does more than tell us when the shark is coming; it sets the emotional mood on which the story is built. Students producing movies, mashups, slide shows, and more would benefit greatly from having access to the music teacher—just another consultant needed by every class.

Theater provides another example. An obvious connection is students producing a play or a short film, but the influence of theater could go much further. Standing in front of a group of people to deliver a keynote presentation, for example, takes an understanding of theater. Delivery and timing are critical in making your point.

In a learning environment in which students are creating real-world products to demonstrate their understanding of the content, the arts faculty becomes a critical network of support, helping to incorporate art and creativity into every subject at every level. Their involvement ensures that our students will develop to the highest level the creative talents critical to their success in life beyond school.

Creativity Fluency in the Real World

It's a little tough to visualize the 5 Is. As we said, it's a whole-brain process, so a real-world example should help illustrate what they look like in practice.

Jordan owns a small graphic design firm and has a wide range of clients. One day, she gets a call from Jeremy and Sarah. They are opening a new restaurant called *Quattro* and are looking for a corporate identity package. Sarah indicates that their biggest concern is the logo, and they want to proceed with designing that first. If Jordan and her team are able to come up with a concept that works, they will get the contract for the rest of the design work.

Identify

Jordan asks them to describe the restaurant. Jeremy launches into his monologue about service and quality of food, and what a unique dining experience it will be. Jordan listens patiently and then begins to ask probing questions to lead the client.

She wants to know what demographic the restaurant is designed for. Is it a buffet-style restaurant for senior citizens? A family restaurant? A steakhouse or sushi joint? Sarah explains that it is a restaurant targeting 17- to 30-year-olds, young people and young professionals, with a combination of Italian and new American cuisine. Then, Jordan asks them to describe the restaurant in a single word. Jeremy says "funky."

This is what Jordan was looking for: descriptive adjectives such as *funky, fresh, young, hip, colorful, stylish, upscale, urban*, and so forth. There are also technical production elements to be considered, which would limit the design, so Jordan asks where the logo will be used.

Does it need to be embroidered or screen-printed? Does the restaurant have an existing color palette to be considered?

Inspire and Interpolate

Jordan sits down with her design team and recaps the meeting. One wall of the design firm is a giant whiteboard they use for production meetings. Up at the top they write *Quattro*. Then, they list the words that describe the look and feel: *funky, young, colorful, stylish, upscale*, and *urban*.

In its basic form, a logo could be considered a font, a color, and a shape. They begin with color for inspiration and start poring over a massive book with Pantone color chips. They suggest colors, comparing them to the words that were identified. Royal blue—not funky. Dark blood red–not upscale. How about Caribbean orange—yes! Electric blue—oh yeah!

Pretty soon several color chips appear on the board for them to draw from. The team is actually toggling back and forth between Inspire and Interpolate, narrowing down the possibilities and avoiding the mental clutter.

Next, they move on to fonts. They type the restaurant's name in big letters projected on the art board. Again, they are seeking a font that will make a good match. Times New Roman—not young. Comic sans—not a good choice. (Let's just delete this font from everyone's computer, okay?) Although they have only been at this for a few hours, they have already started to make good progress and found some very stylish fonts with great potential: Brass Monkey, Madrid, and Brie Light are among the ones that make the cut.

BRASS MONKEY

Madrid

Brie Light

Imagine

The team bounces ideas around. They decide to explore shape and size next. They change the layout of the lettering by using a massive Q with *Quattro* written in the middle. Then they try several other configurations. Some look good, but none seems to really stand out.

Then Robert, a promising young designer, jumps up and says, "I've got it!" He draws four squares in four different colors and writes the word *Quattro* across them. Everyone loves it, it looks amazing, and they think the client will be pleased.

Inspect

The team looks back at their original criteria. Is this logo funky? Is it young, colorful, stylish, upscale, and urban? Can it be embroidered? The team decides it does meet the criteria, but some of the other ideas would work as well, so they assemble a portfolio of possibilities to show the client.

More Real-World Examples

The scenario of developing a logo is an example of using creativity fluency to develop an artistic product. We've used this example because we wanted to demonstrate that developing an artistic product such as a logo is within the reach of anyone. Carefully applying the 5 Is of Creativity Fluency will guide you through the process.

Creativity is about more than being able to develop an artistic product. To create or to innovate means to bring something into existence that did not exist before. People capable of lateral thinking, of developing innovative solutions, are what businesses are looking for today. In difficult economic times, visionary thinkers invest in innovation. Here are some examples of successful innovations:

In the 1920s, Post™ and Kellogg's™ brands were the two major competing companies for packaged cereal. A few years later, in the midst of the Great Depression, Post reacted by cutting spending in every area possible. At the same time, Kellogg's invested an enormous amount of money to introduce Rice Krispies™. Their profits rose by over 30 percent, and they eventually became the largest cereal brand in America.

In the 1930s, Brazilian coffee producers had a significant problem: a massive surplus of coffee and a new crop on the way. They desperately needed to expand their market, so they asked Nestlé™ to develop a product from their surplus coffee that was soluble in water but still retained its flavor. The result was the invention of instant coffee, and Nescafé™ became a great success around the world.

Just a few years ago, in 2001, the NASDAQ dropped 30 percent as the Internet bubble burst, only a few months before the September 11 attacks. It was a difficult year for the markets and investors. In the face of low consumer confidence, Procter & Gamble launched Crest WhiteStrips, a resounding success as it rapidly became a $200-million product.

In that same difficult year, Steve Jobs, in an interview in *Rolling Stone*, said, "We decided to innovate our way through this downturn, so that we would be further ahead of our competitors when things turn up." (Jeff Godell, 2003— http://www.scribd.com/doc/60014670/Steve-Jobs-Interview). Apple released the first-generation iPod, which, several iterations later, still holds over 70 percent market share for digital music players.

Each of these success stories happened because of a process similar to Creativity Fluency: identifying the problem, sourcing inspiration, constantly interpolating to focus on relevancy to the market and the problem before finding inspiration in an idea which, when inspected, aligns with the needs of the market and the original problem.

creativity
fluency

Creativity Fluency Snapshot

To help you evaluate the level of proficiency that you or your students have with Creativity Fluency, use this tool. You can use it with individual students or with groups.

There are 10 statements below for you to consider. As you move through the statements, chose a value you feel represents the how well the individual or group you are evaluating has demonstrated the characteristic. Rate each statement from 1 (*strongly disagree*) to 5 (*strongly agree*). Better still, have your students assess themselves and discuss the outcome.

Move down the list, and then add up your total and multiply it by 2. This is the student's Creativity Fluency percentage, which you record in the box provided at the end of each list. From there, you can compare your results in each fluency to determine where focus and improvement may be needed.

Identify
Inspire
Interpolate
Imagine
Inspect

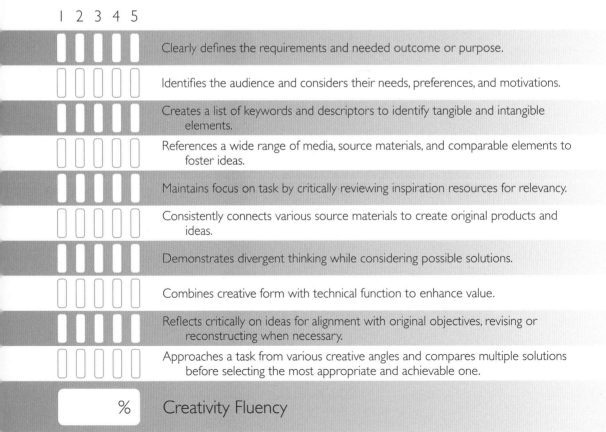

1 2 3 4 5

Clearly defines the requirements and needed outcome or purpose.

Identifies the audience and considers their needs, preferences, and motivations.

Creates a list of keywords and descriptors to identify tangible and intangible elements.

References a wide range of media, source materials, and comparable elements to foster ideas.

Maintains focus on task by critically reviewing inspiration resources for relevancy.

Consistently connects various source materials to create original products and ideas.

Demonstrates divergent thinking while considering possible solutions.

Combines creative form with technical function to enhance value.

Reflects critically on ideas for alignment with original objectives, revising or reconstructing when necessary.

Approaches a task from various creative angles and compares multiple solutions before selecting the most appropriate and achievable one.

% Creativity Fluency

Creativity Fluency
Lesson Plan Grading Tool

The Lesson Plan Grading Tools are used to determine the degree of application of each of the 21st-century fluencies within the context of a unit plan. The Fluency Matrix is located on the front page of every unit plan. It is represented by a vertical line of colorful fluency icons that represent each of the 21st-century fluencies.

Below are a series of statements for you to consider that help to define the characteristics of Creativity Fluency within the context of a unit. Beside each statement is a 1 to 5 scale similar to the ones found in the Fluency Snapshot. As you work through each statement, consider the extent of its application in the unit, and rate each statement from 1 (*strongly disagree*) to 5 (*strongly agree*).

Move down the list, and then add your total up and multiply it by 2. This is the Creativity Fluency percentage, which is an estimation of how effectively a unit plan focuses on it's development in your students.

Identify
Inspire
Interpolate
Imagine
Inspect

	1	2	3	4	5
The challenge/problem requires a unique and creative solution.	☐	☐	☐	☐	☐
The challenge requires students to clearly identify the desired outcome and criteria for achieving it.	☐	☐	☐	☐	☐
The challenge inspires a thought process geared toward creating a unique and innovative solution.	☐	☐	☐	☐	☐
The challenge leads students to gain inspiration and ideas from various sources.	☐	☐	☐	☐	☐
The challenge provides opportunities for utilizing creative digital and non-digital literacies in storytelling, musical, or artistic applications to the problem.	☐	☐	☐	☐	☐
The challenge provides opportunities involving the use of imagination to discover original ideas or concepts used in the production of a creative work.	☐	☐	☐	☐	☐
The challenge requires students to repeatedly revisit, rework, and revise the process at each stage in order to improve the solution.	☐	☐	☐	☐	☐
The challenge requires students to make proper use of a variety of creative digital and non-digital techniques in their solutions.	☐	☐	☐	☐	☐
The solution can be adapted or applied to different creative frameworks and approaches.	☐	☐	☐	☐	☐
The challenge requires students to look at the effectiveness of the product or solution, and reflect on its strengths/weaknesses as an original creative work.	☐	☐	☐	☐	☐

Creativity Fluency %

Summarizing the Main Points

- While IQ scores have gone up about 3 points every decade, creativity scores from the Torrance Tests of Creative Thinking (TTCT) have been plummeting downward since 1990. This decline in scores is primarily happening in the United States.

- Creativity is the currency of the 21st century. Creative individuals and nations are poised to prosper. The new Third World will be the nations that have to import creativity. Businesses are turning to creativity like never before.

- Just as technical proficiency can be taught, so can the creative process. It's a whole-brain process that involves both hemispheres working together using the 5 Is of Creativity Fluency.

- The 5 Is of Creativity Fluency are: Identify, Inspire, Interpolate, Imagine, and Inspect.

- In a learning environment in which students are creating real-world products to demonstrate their understanding of the content, the arts faculty becomes a critical network of support, helping to incorporate art and creativity into every subject at every level.

- Creativity is about more than being able to develop an artistic product. To create or to innovate means to bring something into existence that did not exist before. People capable of lateral thinking, of developing innovative solutions, are what businesses are looking for today. In difficult economic times, visionary thinkers invest in innovation.

Questions to Consider

- How is the current educational process prohibiting creativity? How does standardized testing prohibit it?

- What is the difference between creativity and technical proficiency?

- What are some ways creativity aid students studying math, science, or other traditionally "technical" subjects?

Chapter 7

Media Fluency

> **The medium is the message.**
>
> Marshall McLuhan

Why Is Media Fluency Important?

The most powerful technology for communication used to be the printing press. Today we have a vast array of readily accessible and relatively inexpensive digital tools, ranging from cell phones to computers, that allow us to produce visual and audiovisual content. As a result, we are becoming a visual society, moving beyond just text-based communication.

For generations, graphics have been generally static illustrations, photos, or diagrams that accompanied text and provided some kind of clarification. Think about looking at a paper-based *Encyclopedia Britannica* or the *Book of Knowledge*. They contain massive blocks of text sprinkled with a few photos and illustrations. The very word *illustration* says it all—something that helps to illustrate the point. The primary information was provided by text, and the images were intended to complement that text.

But today, and especially for digital learners, the relationship is almost completely reversed. The role of text has become to provide more detail to something that is first experienced as an image or a video. This is one of the attributes we described in our book *Understanding the Digital Generation*. The digital generation has been continuously exposed since childhood to television, videos, and computer games that deliver colorful, high-quality, highly expressive images and multisensory experiences with little or no accompanying text.

As a result, to the digital generation, images and video are powerful enough on their own to communicate messages. The role of words is merely to complement the images.

While teachers and parents may use Google to look for written information, video is so central to the digital generation that it has become their preferred information source. In fact, YouTube's search service now receives the world's second largest number of search queries per month, and more than 48 hours of video is uploaded every minute.

During the time of Plato, about 2,500 years ago, there was much debate over the value of the oral tradition as we moved from orality to literacy. The momentum, however, was unstoppable, and it altered our lives irrevocably. Today, as we communicate increasingly in environments with little to no text, similar debates are raging. However, multimedia communication is a reality today and will continue to be in the future.

Just as the move from orality to literacy created the need for us to understand how to communicate effectively with the written word, today's shift to multimedia also requires a new understanding. In schools, we need to move beyond our focus on text and expand to include visual media. We need to rethink what our definition of *literate* is, because a person who is literate by the standards of the 20th century may be illiterate in the culture of the 21st century.

It's critical for educators to understand that excellent traditional writing skills are not enough to make someone a good communicator in our multimedia world. Effective communication in the digital age requires more than the ability to produce traditional products like handwritten or typed reports.

The Internet is a wasteland of content developed by people with either very little or no understanding of the principles of design. Proficiency with the elements of graphic design, color theory, harmony, balance, and white space are as foundational to communicating today as an understanding of dramatic structure with its exposition, climax, and denouement.

We live in an interactive visual world. We all must be able to create and publish original digital products that help us communicate effectively with text, visual, and auditory elements. Students today need to be able to communicate as effectively in graphical formats as we were taught to communicate with text.

The Process

People often think Media Fluency means being proficient with various technologies, but it is much more than this. Media fluency goes beyond operating a digital camera or knowing how to create a podcast. It's about being able to look critically at content in any medium, but it also involves choosing the most appropriate and effective medium for communicating an intended message and then being able to produce it.

Media Fluency means being a "prosumer"—an effective consumer and producer of digital content. So there are two components for Media Fluency: one for media input, or consuming, and another for media output, or producing.

Listening

Listening is not just an auditory skill and not about passive consumption; it means really hearing. It's about being able to look critically at the content of a web site, video, blog, wiki, TV show, newscast, or video game. Listening involves being able to decode the real message in the wide range of media available to the average individual and understanding how messages can be shaped, biased, or even completely misrepresented.

It involves understanding how the media can be used to shape our thinking, and, in addition, evaluating how well a particular medium is being used and considering whether a different one would have been more appropriate.

In other words, listening is about measuring the effectiveness of messages being communicated by the media.

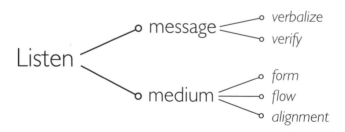

Message—To measure the effectiveness of a message, we must first separate the medium from the message. When all the distractions of the media are removed (the explosions, the heavy metal guitars, the screeching tires, etc.), what is really being communicated? What are the originators of the message really saying to you? Are they trying to tell you that if you use this brand of body spray or hair gel, you will be irresistible to the opposite sex? Perhaps it's a political ad telling you all about the dangers in voting for the opposition.

Verbalize—You must be able to verbalize the message clearly and concisely. Being able to do this is essential if you are to avoid becoming a victim of media and are instead to be able to think critically, analytically, and independently.

Verify—Second, it is imperative that you verify the message. This will require skills from Information Fluency, analyzing and authenticating, separating fact from opinion, and detecting bias. Verifying does not mean determining if the message is true, though that certainly is part of it. It is perfectly acceptable that the message be an opinion, but if it is, it must be identified as such and considered appropriately. If it is presented as a fact, then what are the sources? Are they verifiable? If not, perhaps it is opinion masquerading as fact.

Verbalizing and verifying, when applied appropriately, allow you to understand the true message and to be separated from the influence of well-crafted media.

Medium—Now that you have a grasp of the message, you can consider the medium, which involves an analysis of the physical delivery as well as evaluation of the efficacy and appropriateness of the chosen medium.

Form—There are three aspects to evaluating the medium. The first is considering form. This is primarily about the design: the elements of design and methods for its analysis are too lengthy to present here, but they include color scheme, font, unity, balance, white space, lighting, and so forth. All these elements must reflect the message and work together harmoniously. In some cases, there may be intentional stress and imbalance intended to create a sense of discomfort. What is important is that when designed appropriately, the elements of the form should be able to communicate the message on their own, and the words, if present, will be secondary.

Flow—Everything has flow. A great story has a flow. The main characters are introduced, the scene is set, the tension builds, a climax is reached, and the denouement unfolds as the conflict is resolved. A movie has a flow, and everyone has seen a movie that started off great but then fell apart in the middle as the flow was lost. Great paintings have flow. They are created to move your eyes to specific points of focus. Display ads also have a flow. Building on the principles of the masters of the Renaissance and translated to the digital tools of today, design firms and advertising agencies make millions of dollars creating works that draw your attention and pull you through the message in the sea of interruption marketing in which we are drowning today.

As you look at the medium, ask yourself, is there a logical progression from beginning to end? If the flow is good, the synergy of the medium and the message will greatly enhance the message, making it something more than it would be on its own.

Students today need to be able to communicate as effectively in graphical formats as we were taught to communicate with text.

Alignment—Finally, you must consider the alignment. There is an unbreakable trinity between the medium, the message, and the audience. If they are not in alignment, the message will be ineffective, or it will be less effective than it could be.

Consider the intended audience and the purpose of this communication. Does the medium align with the message, and has the most appropriate medium been chosen? For example, if the intended audience is senior citizens, then creating a viral video with fast motion and Goth death metal music would most likely not be an appropriate medium.

Leverage

Learning how to really listen, how to verbalize and verify the message and analyze the medium for form, flow, and alignment, are foundational in being able to choose the most appropriate medium for producing a message.

This is not about learning technical skills but about learning how to communicate effectively, which means being able to identify the most appropriate medium for getting a message out. For one particular message, a podcast might be the best tool. Other times, a web site might be the most effective, or a video, or perhaps a printed document or an interactive PDF.

Matching the medium to the message and the audience is a critical component of media literacy. Learning about the technology is nothing more than an incidental but essential by-product of the process. The tools will change, and there will always be new tools to learn about and utilize. But the 21st-century fluencies are not about the hardware; they're about the headware. Media Fluency involves developing the skills to communicate effectively in an interactive multimedia world.

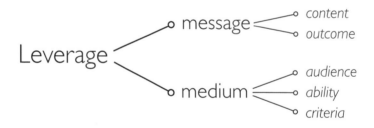

Message—As with listening, you start with the message. There are two elements to consider, and both must be defined clearly. One leads to the other, and though they're not always in the same order, they both must be identified. Sometimes the content of the message is known and the desired outcome needs to be considered. Other times, it is the desired outcome that is clear, and the appropriate content then needs to be developed.

Content—Consider what your message is. What is the substance or content of the message? Understanding your message is often the first step. What is it that you want to say?

Outcome—The second consideration is the desired outcome of the message. This plays an important part in crafting the communication because the same information can be presented in different ways, each with its own outcome. We often refer to this as tone. For example, let's imagine that your spouse was supposed to take out the garbage and you want to inform your partner that you did it instead. You could say, "I know you have a lot on your mind and are really distracted and a little overwhelmed today, so I took the garbage out for you. Now let's just have a glass of wine and relax together." Another way might be to say, "Once again you forgot to take out the garbage, so I had to do it. Why can't you remember a simple task like that?"

Both of these communicate the very same information, but they will potentially have completely different outcomes. What you say is often far less important than how you say it, so the desired outcome needs to be carefully considered.

Medium—With an understanding of the content and the purpose as the foundation, we can then consider the medium and build on the foundation of the message by identifying three additional components

Audience—First, consider who your audience is. Remember the Goth death metal and your grandmother? Who your audience is is an essential component in choosing the most appropriate medium. You may have multiple demographics to consider. For example, you may need to communicate to a broad cross-section of society, men and women, multiple age-groups, or several cultures or income levels. Each component must be considered, and in fact, multiple messages, each designed for a specific group, may be necessary.

Abilities—Second, you have to consider who you are. In other words, what are your abilities? Which media are you capable of using now, and which others are within your grasp? Are you capable of developing new skills though this process? Is it feasible to have someone else do the production for you? Understanding who you are and what is possible for you to achieve will help narrow the list of potential media.

Criteria—Finally, what criteria exist? For example, there may be a specific deadline, in which case time would be a factor. There is always a limited budget, which means you'll have to work with what you have. It's also possible that you face limitations in form. You may be required to produce something specific, such as a slide show presentation, that must conform to very specific criteria, and obviously in this case you would have clear direction as to the medium since only a few dozen tools are appropriate for creating a slide show.

With all these elements identified, the content and desired outcome of the message, the demographics of your audience, an understanding of your abilities and options, and any existing criteria, you have everything you need to choose the most appropriate medium.

Your decision as to what medium that is will come from your experience as both a consumer and a producer. By listening, you evaluate the efficacy of different media for communicating specific messages to a range of audiences. Through your own experiences leveraging media, you will gain even more insight into choosing a medium that works well. With a medium selected, you will be ready to use the other fluencies to develop your communication.

So what would be the result of students creating digital products as outcomes that do more than reflect an understanding of the necessary content? If, instead of scripting what they have to do, we ask them to demonstrate what they know and to choose the most appropriate method in which to communicate, what would they produce? Imagine it! The possibilities are endless!

Our students would be inspired and engaged, and they would probably use current technology differently than we would, in unanticipated ways, to create unexpected products. In fact, this is usually the outcome we experience when we work with educators around the globe. The classroom becomes an inspiring place to be for both the teacher and the students.

A few years ago, we worked with a group of teachers in rural Arkansas. One of those teachers, Sarah, was in her late 50s and quite set in her ways as a teacher. However, she had come to realize that what had always worked in the classroom wasn't working anymore and that for the sake of her students, she needed to do something different. Although she had considerable anxiety over making the shift to a 21st-century learning environment, she embraced the process, knowing there would be bumps along the road.

We met Sarah a year later at a regional conference. She bounded up to the stage to speak with us, beaming with enthusiasm. When we asked her how things were going in her classroom, she said, "My students shock and amaze me every day. Do you know what a green screen is? Well, I'd never heard of it before. My students brought in this bolt of fabric and starting shooting a video about a time traveler going back in time to research how people lived before electricity. I am so excited to go to school; I never know what they are going to do, but attendance is perfect, I rarely have any discipline issues, and their test scores are up dramatically."

This is not an isolated incident. It is the usual response we hear from educators who have stopped scripting learning and are giving students the opportunity to communicate what they know and what they have learned in a way that speaks to them. In our multimedia world, communication isn't just about text anymore. Our students need Media Fluency to understand how to be more effective in using their digital tools to solve problems and create real-life products that communicate, inspire, and entertain.

Media Fluency in the Real World

It's Friday night, and it's been a long, tiring week. The city is normally warm and vibrant, but tonight it's windy, cold, and a little rainy. Jeremy and Ashley normally go out after dinner for a walk, but tonight is just one of those nights that the couch drains the energy from their legs and multiplies the gravity, making them feel as if they're on Jupiter and getting up would be a struggle. They give in and turn on the television.

As on most nights, there are 150 channels of absolutely nothing, and in an attempt to find some form of entertainment, they go channel by channel discussing what is wrong with each show and what they would do if they were studio executives for a day. "Why do they call it reality television?" poses Jeremy. "Putting a bunch of people on an island with the sole purpose of backstabbing each other for money. How can it be reality when people know there are cameras on them? How is it that they sleep in huts with no running water but manage to have makeup and hair done? Look, you can see where the makeup crew has strategically applied dirt to make them look shipwrecked." Ashley contributes, "The only thing that is reality television is sports. When the Miami Heat beats the Lakers, that's not scripted, it's poetry. I can't help it; I just love Dwayne Wade!"

"Hey, why is it each one of these cooking competition shows has at least one person that's supposed to be a chef, but doesn't know how to cook scrambled eggs? Where do they find these people?" Ashley asks rhetorically. "Probably from the bistro we had dinner at last week," says Jeremy. "Oh yeah, that was not a happy-tummy experience."

Listen

Then they change the channel, and there is a commercial in which a nerdy-looking guy with a pencil-thin tie, black glasses, and the obligatory pocket protector is looking in the mirror at his hair. He takes a handful of some orange goop from a black jar and smears it on his head, transforming his hair into the latest whimsical style. Instantly, the doorbell rings. He opens the door to three stunning women, who pounce on him like a pack of hyenas. "I'm buying some of that tomorrow," Jeremy announces. "It won't work. I'm not going to jump on you like that, and the doorbell won't be ringing, either," Ashley remarks.

Then they enter into a discussion about this advertisement. They talk about what the message is and decide that even though it is humorous and obviously farcical, it is implying that beautiful women will be uncontrollably drawn to any guy who uses this gel. They talk about the fact that the company has stated nothing about the quality or advantages of its product. In fact, they have stated nothing in the ad—absolutely nothing.

The desired outcome must be to associate the product with the transformation that everyone is familiar with—the shift from feeling uncomfortable and a bit of an outcast to being able to connect with the opposite sex.

Although the ad states nothing and uses humor to be disarming, the company is trying to connect with those subconscious insecurities many of us have. Jeremy and Ashley then go on to talk about the medium and how communicating this kind of message without words is most effective in a moving visual form and that a display ad in a magazine wouldn't be anywhere near as effective. After Ashley reassures Jeremy that he is all the man she could ever want, he decides he doesn't need the gel, and they continue to home renovation shows.

Leverage

Every morning before class, Tanya goes for a run. Right in the middle of the city are a group of trails that wander along the riverside. The views are beautiful, but increasingly, she is noticing more and more garbage appearing in the woods and along the river. One morning, she has had enough and decides that someone has to do something.

She knows that she wants to get the area cleaned up and keep it clean and that she'll need help to make it happen. She starts thinking about who would help. The trails are used by so many people who must share her feelings—runners, students walking to class, nature lovers—but how can she reach them all?

She decides on multiple approaches. First, she creates a Facebook page and invites her friends to join and invite their friends. She also speaks to the local running store and the local outdoor store; both send the link to their email lists. Someone from the running club suggests that they do a run-and-pick workout, where each person runs to a different point on the trail with a garbage bag and then walks, picking up all the trash they find until they reach where the next person started.

There are many miles of trails, though, more than the running club could handle. She posts the event to her Facebook page and invites everyone. She gets confirmed responses from dozens of people, more than enough to make it work: students, runners, people from the outdoor store, and people that joined the page after seeing a link on a friend's page.

However, Tanya wants to address the trash issue long-term, and because there are no trash barrels along the trail, she thinks the problem is likely to continue. She could just organize an annual cleanup, but watching garbage accumulate over the next year would be very discouraging—it's not a permanent solution to the problem.

She takes a photo of the trail with all the garbage and layers a trash barrel on top, with an empty white square with the text "Your logo here" and arrows pointing from the trash to the barrel with the text "All this garbage in here." She puts together a simple brochure with some additional copy asking for sponsorship of the trash barrels and drops copies off to businesses near the trail. The barrels sell quickly, and she raises more than enough money to get them produced. Then she realizes that the problem will be getting the barrels emptied.

She asks for suggestions from her Facebook group. One of the members who joined the list from the outdoor store also happens to be the leader of a local Boy Scout troop that is always looking for fundraising and service opportunities.

The leftover funds from the barrel sponsorship go to the Boy Scout troop, who take over the entire program, emptying the barrels and arranging for sponsorship renewals each year. Now when Tanya goes for a run, instead of frustration over the garbage, she is filled with a sense of pride as she runs past the barrels.

media
fluency

Listen
Leverage

Media Fluency Snapshot

To help you evaluate the level of proficiency that you or your students have with Media Fluency, use this tool. You can use it with individual students or with groups.

There are 10 statements below for you to consider. As you move through the statements, chose a value you feel represents the how well the individual or group you are evaluating has demonstrated the characteristic. Rate each statement from 1 (*strongly disagree*) to 5 (*strongly agree*). Better still, have your students assess themselves and discuss the outcome.

Move down the list, and then add up your total and multiply it by 2. This is the student's Media Fluency percentage, which you record in the box provided at the end of each list. From there, you can compare your results in each fluency to determine where focus and improvement may be needed.

1 2 3 4 5

Understands how a wide range of media and designs shape opinions and inspire emotions.

Identifies the audience and considers their needs, preferences, and motivations.

Selects the most appropriate media from a wide range for effectively communicating with various audiences.

Accurately and consistently discerns the intended message from a wide range of media.

Verifies the accuracy of the message, identifying fact, bias, opinion, and slant.

Discerns alignment in the application of media to a message and purpose in a variety of formats.

Defines the purpose of a communication and considers how the form of a message influences the outcome.

Has an understanding of the principles of graphic design and employs them creatively.

Consistently shares and presents ideas effectively using a variety of media platforms.

Critically reviews and adjusts the communication as necessary to ensure alignment with the audience, message, and purpose.

%   Media Fluency

Media Fluency
Lesson Plan Grading Tool

The Lesson Plan Grading Tools are used to determine the degree of application of each of the 21st-century fluencies within the context of a unit plan. The Fluency Matrix is located on the front page of every unit plan. It is represented by a vertical line of colorful fluency icons that represent each of the 21st-century fluencies.

Below are a series of statements for you to consider that help to define the characteristics of Media Fluency within the context of a unit. Beside each statement is a 1 to 5 scale similar to the ones found in the Fluency Snapshot. As you work through each statement, consider the extent of its application in the unit and rate each statement from 1 (*strongly disagree*) to 5 (*strongly agree*).

Move down the list, and then add your total up and multiply it by 2. This is the Media Fluency percentage, which is an estimation of how effectively a unit plan focuses on it's development in your students.

Listen
Leverage

	1	2	3	4	5
The challenge requires students to analyze various media to extract messages and meaning from their usage.					
The challenge encourages students to listen actively when viewing different media to decode the messages that the media are sending to viewers.					
The challenge encourages students to consider how different media are used to shape thinking and opinions.					
The challenge encourages students to consider how media can be used harmfully, inappropriately, or to misrepresent information.					
The challenge requires students to consider a range of digital media when creating a solution.					
The challenge requires students to incorporate a digital product into their solution.					
The problem/challenge requires students to justify the choice of the media used and why it was selected.					
The challenge guides students to consider their audience, purpose, and abilities when choosing the appropriate media for delivery of their intended solution.					
The challenge requires students to analyze the intended message in their media for form, flow, and alignment with the intended audience and purpose.					
The challenge guides students into a critical reflection and evaluation of the product created and the process undertaken in developing their solution.					

Media Fluency   %

⚙ Summarizing the Main Points

- We are becoming a visual society, moving beyond just text-based communication. The digital generation has been continuously exposed since childhood to television, videos, and computer games that deliver colorful, high-quality, highly expressive images and multisensory experiences with little or no accompanying text. As a result, to the digital generation, images and video are powerful enough on their own to communicate messages. The role of words is merely to complement the images.

- A person who is literate by the standards of the 20th century may be illiterate in the culture of the 21st century.

- Media Fluency means being a "prosumer"—an effective consumer and producer of digital content.

- Media Fluency (Listen and Leverage) involves developing the skills to communicate effectively in an interactive multimedia world.

- Students need Media Fluency to understand how to be more effective in using their digital tools to solve problems and create real-life products that communicate, inspire, and entertain.

⚙ Questions to Consider

- How would you define literacy in the 21st century?

- Can you think of an example where your message was not matching the medium?

Chapter 8

Collaboration Fluency

> Coming together is a beginning. Keeping together is progress. Working together is success.
>
> Henry Ford

Global virtual communication is now a reality, and this is having an enormous impact on daily life. Kids seeking information or playing games today are just as likely to interact with, compete against, and collaborate with people from Europe and Asia as they are to interact with people from North America.

Electronic technology in wired, and wireless communications has quite literally meant the death of distance. There has never been a time in which distance has meant less than it does today. Students learning about civil war could be talking directly with kids in Serbia or Afghanistan. Kids trying to understand the impact of oil spills could talk with students in Louisiana, Mississippi, or Florida. Students wanting to understand the impact of natural disasters such as earthquakes and tsunamis could talk to students in Japan or New Zealand.

Students today can work in virtual partnerships on projects with kids from across town or across the world, and the skills they develop will help them greatly because the working world is being affected by new communication technology as well.

One of our recent books, *The Digital Diet*, was written by Andrew Churches, Lee Crockett, and Ian Jukes. At the time of its writing, Lee was living in Kyoto, Japan, while Andrew was living near Auckland, New Zealand, and Ian was wandering here and there across the globe.

Yet, despite the fact that they were never in the same room at the same time until they met sometime later at a conference in Denver, Colorado, they successfully wrote the book *The Digital Diet*.

Not only that, but each also met and knew well the others' wives and children. How did they do this? Using Skype and a wide range of online software.

This is the essence of modern-day collaboration. It's about much more than students sitting around a table working to solve a problem.

We define Collaboration Fluency as team-working proficiency characterized by the unconscious ability to work cooperatively with both real and virtual partners in both physical and virtual environments to solve real and simulated problems.

The Process

Establish

Collaboration fluency starts by establishing several key components.

The group—defining the collective, identifying stakeholders, and assembling the group.

Roles and responsibilities—determining the areas of interest and expertise; assigning the most effective roles for each team member; describing specific responsibilities for each member of the group; determining the level of ownership and control group members have; stating how the group will make decisions when they can't reach agreement; setting time frames on what gets done when; establishing a process for handling disagreements within the group; deciding how the group will determine accountability; and stating what will happen if a group member is not demonstrating accountability.

Norms—determining how communication will take place and how often members need to communicate with one another and establishing what the norms of the group will be, why the collective has been established, what the outcome will be, and how that outcome will be evaluated.

Defining the scope of the project—framing the challenge or issues the group will address; identifying the stakeholders; identifying the project expectations; and defining success and the desired results.

Information needs—specifying what available and needed information is pertinent to the issue.

Leadership—stating who the leader(s) of this collaborative process are and what the scope of their responsibility is.

Group contract—establishing the performance expectations for each member of the group and signing a group contract. This involves identifying each group member's roles and responsibilities and defining the established norms and the outcome.

This becomes the solid foundation for you to Envision.

Envision

According to Merriam-Webster's online dictionary, *envision* means to see something in your mind, usually to imagine the form or appearance of something that is not yet real. For example, you might envision a scene, such as how a room would look when painted or decorated, or envision a form of life on another planet or the future if some change were made to the present.

At the Envision stage of Collaboration Fluency, the group visualizes, defines, and examines the purpose, issue, challenge, preferred solution, or goal as a group and collectively develops an agreement as to what the outcome of the collaboration will be as well as what criteria will be used to evaluate the outcome. The critical elements are:

- Defining the problem
- Defining the current situation
- Defining the desired future
- Specifying the information needs
- Identifying the information that is available and what is needed
- Educating the rest of the collective (again, and whenever it is needed)
- Developing a written plan of action: what, how, when, where, and who

The critical element here is the dual focus placed on envisioning an outcome and the collaborative processes that will be utilized to successfully achieve the envisioned outcome. And remember, we must always keep in mind that this is not a linear process. As our understanding of things evolves, we will likely need to revisit every previous stage of this as well as all of the other fluencies.

Establish and Envision lead naturally to the next step, which is to Engineer a plan.

Engineer

Engineering a workable plan means breaking out all the necessary steps to get us from where we are to where we want to be. The essential Engineer skills include delegating responsibilities to each team member for the most efficient and engaging process and creating a plan to guide us as we work—a plan that can be checked and discussed and re-evaluated on an ongoing basis.

This is a parallel process to what we have described with Design in Solution Fluency. The critical element is to allow each member's personal strengths, insight, and creativity to contribute to the process. And it is essential that all this groundwork be done before commencing work. With the collective established, the outcome envisioned, and the plan engineered, it's time to Execute.

Execute

Execute is a parallel process to Deliver in Solution Fluency. Here the plan is put into action with a focus on the development of a tangible, viable solution or product that best utilizes the individual strengths of the various members of the collective. As with Deliver, developing a theoretical solution is only half the task.

The solution then has to be pressure-tested. Designing a presentation isn't enough; it has to be presented. Without fully implementing a solution, the group will never know if it will work. Seeing the product delivered gives each member of the group valuable information and feedback, both personally and collectively.

Finally, there is Examine. Once executed, the most valuable insights are gained by taking time to Examine the process undertaken and the product or solution created.

Examine

Examine involves looking back at the process and determining as a group if the challenge was met and the goal achieved, looking at areas of improvement, recognizing contributions, and giving constructive feedback and criticism.

Did the various members fulfill their roles and responsibilities? Were the agreed-to norms followed? How were decisions made? How were disagreements handled? How effectively were matters communicated to other members of the collective? Were project deadlines and group and individual performance expectations met?

The collaboration isn't complete and the collective can't be dissolved until after a thorough examination and an agreement that all of the elements of the group contract have been fulfilled.

Collaboration Fluency in the Real World

Members of the Glennrochon Middle School community were shocked to hear about the earthquake and tsunami in Japan. The tragedy was particularly powerful because the school was hosting five Japanese exchange students from a village in the Fukushima region of the country. Several parents, including all five who were sponsoring

The critical element here is the dual focus placed on envisioning an outcome and the collaborative processes that will be utilized to successfully achieve the envisioned outcome.

the exchange students, approached the administration, teachers, and staff of the school with the idea of holding a fundraising event for the victims of the disaster.

Principal Mary Turner, secretary Anna Brown, PE teacher Jeremy Ito, and Grade 8 math teacher Larry Wells volunteered to work with the parents (Rob Sinclair, Betty and Mike Green, Russell Peters, Tina Mohan, Janet Prentice, and Mika Kelly) to form a committee to organize the event.

Establish

On a warm, sunny May evening, the committee had its first meeting at Mary's house. The first order of business was introductions, followed by suggestions as to what they hoped to accomplish.

Initially the thought was to have a bake sale, hold a raffle, and organize other separate events to raise money. As the conversation continued, though, the committee realized there was a great opportunity not only to raise money but also to celebrate Japanese culture. In the end, it was agreed that the fundraising day would be more than just a few fundraising events; it would be a day of fun for the whole family, with lots of activities and displays, including judo, karate, and kendo demonstrations; a Japanese quiz; a handmade accessories sale; sushi demonstrations and sales; calligraphy and postcards; an origami demonstration; Japanese music; Japanese cakes and green tea; Japanese hair and beauty treatment demonstrations; a bouncy castle, trampolines, and an inflatable slide; sports activities; a book stall; a second-hand clothing stall; team-building games and challenges; and more.

Quickly people stepped forward to take on responsibilities. Because he was of Japanese heritage, Jeremy offered to organize the cultural events. Anna, Betty, and Tina offered to assist. Larry, Janet, and Rob offered to set up the sports activities, games, and challenges; and Russell and Mika took charge of the book stall, second-hand sales, and food. Mike agreed to take care of advertising and fundraising; and Anna offered to take care of the finances.

As a team, they set time frames, organized a schedule of follow-up meetings, and agreed on how they would communicate with one another by email and phone.

The different groups then met separately, outlined their tasks, and set out to identify what they already knew and what they needed to find out to start the planning process.

This became a solid foundation for Envision.

Envision

The various groups then worked separately and together to visualize their goal. They came to an understanding of what the outcome of the collaboration would be as well as the criteria they would use to determine their success. To do this, they defined the challenges as well as their desired future, identified their information needs, shared their ideas and challenges with the other groups, and created a written plan of action that specified all the whats hows, wheres, and whos.

As they worked the process, problems, obstacles, and challenges appeared, but working separately and collectively, they worked through them one by one and solved each problem or adjusted their vision, making sure to keep the other members of the committee informed as to how their planning was progressing.

Engineer

With the date of the event rapidly approaching, the entire committee met to provide an overview of the planning to this stage. Working together, they developed a plan for the event, breaking out all the necessary steps to get from where they were to where they wanted to be. As they worked through the process, the committee collectively delegated to each team member his or her responsibilities and created a step-by-step plan to guide the team as they worked through organizing the event.

As they did, several questions related to supplies, supervision, and safety appeared. But because all of the members of the team had been kept informed throughout the planning process, these problems were quickly overcome. Finally, the big day arrived, and it was time to Execute the plan.

Execute

After almost two months of planning and organization, the team put their plans into action. Setup of the fairground was hampered by rain the night before, but because the possibility of bad weather had been anticipated, plans had already been made to move several of the events to the gym and the cafeteria just in case. As it turned out, the weather quickly turned sunny and warm, and by the time the fundraiser was under way, the committee was able to use their original plans. As with Deliver, developing a theoretical solution is only half the task. The solution then has to be pressure-tested. Designing a presentation isn't enough; it has to be presented. It turned out to be a long but very successful day. More than 800 people attended the fundraiser and an astounding $28,000 was raised for UNESCO. More than that, the community came to view Japanese culture in a very different way; and the exchange students were deeply honored by the efforts of the Glennrochon Middle School community to support them and their country.

Finally, the committee met one last time at Mary's house to Examine.

Examine

As they sat in the backyard sipping cold drinks and listening to the sizzle of burgers on the BBQ, the members of the committee looked back over the events of the past few months and reflected on two things. First, the process—they determined as a group whether the challenge had been met and the goal achieved.

Then they discussed areas of improvement, acknowledged contributions, and provided constructive feedback and criticism to the others. While they agreed in retrospect that there were many things they might have done differently had they known then what they knew now, they were in complete agreement that the fundraiser was both a financial and a technical success. They agreed that the planning process had been a good one and decided that they would try to make this an annual event.

collaboration
fluency

Collaboration Fluency Snapshot

To help you evaluate the level of proficiency that you or your students have with Collaboration Fluency, use this tool. You can use it with individual students or with groups.

There are 10 statements below for you to consider. As you move through the statements, chose a value you feel represents the how well the individual or group you are evaluating has demonstrated the characteristic. Rate each statement from 1 (*strongly disagree*) to 5 (*strongly agree*). Better still, have your students assess themselves and discuss the outcome.

Move down the list, and then add up your total and multiply it by 2. This is the student's Collaboration Fluency percentage, which you record in the box provided at the end of each list. From there, you can compare your results in each fluency to determine where focus and improvement may be needed.

Establish
Envision
Engineer
Execute
Examine

1 2 3 4 5

Exhibits skill sets required to organize people/data/resources.

Interacts with others to generate ideas and develop products.

Uses appropriate interpersonal skills within a variety of media and social contexts.

Productively collaborates across networks using various technologies.

Effectively participates as a team member and knows his or her own capacities for filling different team roles.

Demonstrates proficiency in managing personal relationships.

Uses various means to manage conflict.

Understands creative process through collaboration, the exchange of ideas, and building on the achievements of others.

Shows sensitivity to issues and processes associated with collaborating across cultures.

Revisits, reflects critically on, and revises the process and the product at each stage.

%   Collaboration Fluency

Collaboration Fluency
Lesson Plan Grading Tool

The Lesson Plan Grading Tools are used to determine the degree of application of each of the 21st century-fluencies within the context of a unit plan. The Fluency Matrix is located on the front page of every unit plan. It is represented by a vertical line of colorful fluency icons that represent each of the 21st-century fluencies.

Below are a series of statements for you to consider that help to define the characteristics of Collaboration Fluency within the context of a unit. Beside each statement is a 1 to 5 scale similar to the ones found in the Fluency Snapshot. As you work through each statement, consider the extent of its application in the unit, and rate each statement from 1 (*strongly disagree*) to 5 (*strongly agree*).

Move down the list, and then add your total up and multiply it by 2. This is the Collaboration Fluency percentage, which is an estimation of how effectively a unit plan focuses on it's development in your students.

collaboration fluency

Establish
Envision
Engineer
Execute
Examine

	1	2	3	4	5
The problem/challenge requires students to work in teams to create an effective S.M.A.R.T. solution.					
The challenge requires students to interact with team members to share information, exchange opinions, and generate ideas.					
The challenge requires students to practice personal and team management/organizational skills.					
The challenge encourages students to utilize personal strengths and aptitudes for the benefit of the team.					
The challenge encourages input and viewpoints from all team members.					
The challenge encourages students to think laterally where opinions/viewpoints differ and requires strategies for conflict management and mediation.					
The students accept personal responsibility for their own role in team production and peer support/encouragement.					
The challenge encourages collaboration through cross-cultural recognition and sensitivity.					
The challenge requires the solution to be executed with shared participation and management by all team members.					
The challenge guides students into a critical reflection and evaluation of the product created and the process undertaken in developing their solution.					

Collaboration Fluency   %

Summarizing the Main Points

- Global virtual communication is now a reality, and electronic technology in wired and wireless communications has quite literally meant the death of distance.

- Collaboration Fluency is team-working proficiency characterized by the unconscious ability to work cooperatively with both real and virtual partners to solve real and simulated problems.

- The 5 Es of Collaboration Fluency are: Establish, Envision, Engineer, Execute, and Examine.

Questions to Consider

- What are some other ways global virtual communication can be used as a classroom tool for learning?

- How would you define modern-day collaboration?

- Why is a Group Contract important?

Chapter 9
Global Digital Citizenship

> Our species needs, and deserves, a citizenry with minds wide awake and a basic understanding of how the world works.
>
> Carl Sagan

When we cultivate in our students each of the fluencies—the 5 Is of Creativity Fluency, the 6 Ds of Solution Fluency, the 5 Es of Collaboration Fluency, the 5 As of Information Fluency, and the 2 Ls of Media Fluency—we are not only helping them develop the skills they need for the 21st century; we are also helping them to become something more. We are helping them to become an IDEAL that we call the global digital citizen.

Not that long ago, our connection to the rest of the world was through *National Geographic* or small clips of videos on the news. Of course, this is not the case anymore. When we said earlier that even our newspapers arrive out of date, we meant it. Today, world events are narrated in real time online. The Internet and the rise of social media have given us the power to be connected in ways we could not previously have imagined.

They have transformed the political stage, toppled governments, and bypassed censorship. Consider how the struggles of people in Tunisia empowered the people of Egypt to force a regime change, which sparked the actions in Libya.

When the earthquake and tsunami devastated Japan, telephone communication was impossible. We, like many others, relied on social media to communicate with our friends and family there. A friend of Lee's was walking down the street in his hometown of Nara when a major aftershock struck. He quickly tweeted that there had been another earthquake and asked where the epicenter was. At the time, Lee was online, watching a streaming live feed of a Japanese news program. Within a minute of his friend's tweet, Lee responded with information on the location of the epicenter and the magnitude of the quake. This was done in a conversational style, as if they were both in the same room, even though they haven't been in the same room for more than a year! In our digital lives, we stay so connected to our friends it's like we have one long conversation that never ends; it just has some very long pauses. Think about that for a moment.

This level of global interconnectedness is staggering. We are past the time when we can think of ourselves only in terms of our own country. We have all become elevated to the status of global citizens, both socially and as a workforce. As such, we need to understand that we must be able to communicate and collaborate with people of other cultures, both in person and in virtual environments.

Although our actions have always had global and long-lasting impacts, never before have we been able to see them. What happens in Vegas stays on Facebook. Employers and universities are monitoring social media as part of their decision-making processes. There have been many documented cases of employees being terminated as a result of their online activities.

Recently, a riot broke out in Vancouver after a hockey game. Cars were burned, stores were looted, and the whole thing was documented and played out in real time on the Internet. A page was created for people to post photos and videos as a repository for identifying the culprits. The title on the page couldn't be more true: "Anonymous Crime in a Web 2.0 World? I Don't Think So!"

Over one million photos and videos of these actions were uploaded. Universities suspended students identified from the photos. People posted comments bragging about their antics and were quickly fingered by their "friends." The police pressed charges from the hundreds of leads they received.

Vancouver is a beautiful, peaceful, safe, nature-loving city. People do not take kindly to their international reputation being tarnished by a small group of fools. In addition to the online reporting, a Facebook group was spontaneously created and and used to organize a cleanup for the following morning. More than 10,000 Vancouverites showed up at 6 a.m. to clean up and repair the damage, all organized through social media in a few hours.

We are also beginning to recognize the global environmental impact of local decisions. Conversely, world events are affecting policies at home. Within hours of the first reports of trouble with the Fukushima nuclear facility, there were calls for a moratorium on construction of nuclear plants in North America and discussions of how the safety of existing facilities should be re-evaluated. Within a week, fear led to panic, and Geiger counters and iodine pills were trending topics and sold out in many places across the United States.

As we have all become global citizens in a digital world, we need to cultivate within our students a sense of what this means. Global Digital Citizenship becomes the background of core values and personal identity upon which we apply the other fluencies. For example, Solution Fluency may allow you to create a plan for hacking the school computer and changing your grades. Information Fluency may allow you to determine what you need to change your grades to in order to qualify for your university of choice. Creativity Fluency might help you to cover your tracks, developing documents that look authentic. Collaboration Fluency may make the whole process faster by working with the team, whose grades could likewise be improved. However, Global Digital Citizenship is the framework that helps you to consider whether this would be a good idea and an appropriate action to undertake.

In our unit plans, we provide connections to the tenets of Global Digital Citizenship and suggest ways in which these tenets can be cultivated, both during presentation of the unit and after it's over. Because this directly involves the students' lives and actions, there is instant relevance and therefore engagement. At the same time, we are helping students to define and shape their core beliefs.

Personal Responsibility

As parents, part of our job is to ensure that by the time our children leave us, to a certain extent they no longer need us. This also applies to our children as students. Inherent in 21st-century learning is the shifting of responsibility for the learning from the teacher, where it has traditionally been located, to the student, where it should be. It is their learning, and it is they who should be accountable for it. Fostering personal responsibility (how one governs oneself in matters of finance, ethical and moral boundaries, personal health and fitness, and relationships of every definition) is part of this process. This shift in the instructional approach doesn't define these matters for our students; instead, it provides them ample opportunity to define them for themselves.

Global Citizenship

Citizenship is no longer limited to the country in which one resides. The digital media that abound have torn down borders and boundaries, enabling communication, collaboration, dialogue, and debate on a scale never before seen, and across all levels of society.

Previous generations had infrequent opportunities to interact with other cultures, which they did largely though travel or through the limited exposure and points of view provided by mainstream media, usually in the face of conflict or disaster. This generation and those to follow are no longer isolated—they are global citizens. As such, they must become aware of the issues, traditions, religions, and core values and cultures of our fellow global citizens. To do so will require tolerance and understanding, linked intimately with acceptance, sensitivity, and humility. Ultimately, these connections will change the world.

Digital Citizenship

One exceptional opportunity to help cultivate personal responsibility is through a properly implemented program of digital citizenship, which defines appropriate behavior in an online environment. Acceptable use policies that have been the norm previously are mostly lists of rules, the "Thou Shalt Nots" of using technology. They are large, unwieldy documents that constantly require updating as new technologies emerge and students learn to navigate around them.

Obviously, there must be some guidance. The analogy we use is that you wouldn't hand the car keys to your teenager before he or she had been taught how to drive and gotten a license and without some agreement as to his or her behavior while driving. We do, however, hand Internet-enabled digital devices to our children—often at a very early age—with little to no guidance.

While an acceptable use policy seems to be an appropriate solution, what we have found to be much more effective is to shift the accountability for appropriate behavior to the students, which fosters independence and personal responsibility.

We work with students to help them understand appropriate use, and we have them sign on a yearly basis a Digital Citizenship Contract in which they agree to these six main principles:

- Respect themselves.
- Protect themselves.
- Respect others.
- Protect others.
- Respect intellectual property.
- Protect intellectual property.

The disciplinary actions we develop in consultation with districts reflect the real world. For example, illegally downloading music or movies is theft: A student wouldn't walk into a store and steal a DVD or CD, so why would they download one without paying for it? They need to understand that their online self is the same as their real self, and as such, they must act appropriately and deal with the same consequences in both environments.

With the contract in place and explained, the responsibility always comes back to the student. We don't have to create rules—our students must decide if their actions are in line with the principles to which they have committed themselves.

Most of the schools we work with have wide-open Internet, or Internet with very basic filtering in place. As several students have told us, filtering the Internet only makes it difficult for the adults; the students know how to use a proxy server and punch a hole through the filter. In addition, all that's really required is any one of their 3G devices, which are of course completely unfiltered, as is the Internet they use at home and everywhere else. We believe that rather than trying to block the Internet, a better solution is provided through the Digital Citizenship Agreement, which, through their commitment to respecting and protecting themselves, others, and intellectual property, defines their online behavior at all times—both in school and out. We have provided you with samples of two Digital Citizenship agreements, one for middle school and one for high school, on the next two pages. We invite you to copy them and make good use of their guidelines as part of fostering an environment geared toward Global Digital Citizenry in regards to your student's class projects.

By extension, we also recommend allowing students to use their own devices—that is, cell phones, laptops, tablets, and so forth. One-to-one computing would walk into our schools if we would allow it, and doing so would take the strain off the technology budget. Focus on providing an excellent network, let your students use the tools with which they are most familiar, and apply the savings to staff development instead. The Digital Citizenship Agreement governs the use of your students' devices—off task with a cell phone or a pencil is still off task. A cell phone ringing in class takes everyone off task, so it is not respectful of others and therefore is in contradiction with the students' obligations and has an appropriate predefined consequence. Such instances are all highly teachable moments and would serve to cultivate personal responsibility.

Altruistic Service

As Global Citizens, we are all connected in more ways than ever before. These connections must translate to our concern for the well-being of the people with whom we share our world.

The ideals behind altruism apply not only to the people we know but also to those we don't. Too often, we are placed in positions in which we have an opportunity to exercise charity and goodwill for the benefit of others but don't recognize it or do not act. We must learn never to hesitate to lend our hands or hearts when truly needed.

Altruistic Service provides an excellent opportunity to create relevance and meaningful connections to the real world for our students. While studying a unit on earthquakes, a natural tie-in is through Altruistic Service, which could involve fundraising, joining the local Red Cross, donating blood, building preparedness kits for shut-ins, or connecting with a partner school in an affected area and supporting its needs directly. There are many opportunities to make these connections in any well-crafted unit, and these can be included as an extension of the unit or as part of the unit itself.

Environmental Stewardship

Environmental stewardship is a demonstration not only of commonsense values but also of an appreciation for the beauty and majesty that surrounds us every day.

We only have one world to live in, and we must shepherd and manage our use of its resources, taking responsibility and action on personal, local, regional, national, and international levels. It is important that we consider in advance the true implications of our actions on a global and environmental level as part of our decision-making process.

21st Century Fluency Project

Digital Citizenship Senior School Agreement

Looking After Yourself

- Choosing online names that are suitable and respectful.
- Only inviting people you actually know in the real world to be your friends in the online world.
- Only visiting sites that are appropriate and respecting the rules that web sites have about age. Some sites are only for adults. If you wouldn't feel comfortable showing the web site to you parents or grandparents then its inappropriate.
- Setting your privacy settings so only the people you know can see you and your personal information.
- Only putting information online that is appropriate and posting pictures that are suitable. Not everyone seeing your profile or pictures will be friendly.
- Always reporting anything that happens online which makes you feel uncomfortable or unhappy.
- Talking to trusted adults, like your parents and teachers, about your online experiences. This includes both the good and the bad experiences.

Looking After Others

- Show you care by not flaming (sending hurtful or inflammatory messages) other people, or forwarding messages that are unkind or inappropriate.
- By not getting involved in conversations that are unkind, mean or bullying.
- By reporting any conversations you see that are unkind, mean or bullying. Imagine if the things being written were about you. If you would find them offensive then they are inappropriate.
- Some web sites are disrespectful because they show people behaving inappropriately or illegally—or are racist, bigoted or unkind. Show your respect for others by avoiding these sites. If you visit one by accident, close it and tell your teacher or an adult.
- Show respect for other's privacy by not trying to get into their online spaces without invitation, by not stalking them or copying their pictures.

Looking After Property

- By not stealing other people's property. It's easy to download music, games and movies, but piracy (downloading media that you have not bought) is just the name given to stealing online.
- By not sharing the music, movies, games and other software that you own with other people.
- By checking that the information you are using is correct. Anyone can say anything on the web, so you need to check that the research is correct by using reliable sites. When in doubt ask your teacher or your parents.
- By looking after other people's web sites, acting appropriately when visiting them, not making changes or vandalizing them, and reporting any damage that you finds.

By signing this agreement, I undertake to always act in a manner that is respectful to myself and others, and to act appropriately, and in a moral and ethical manner.

I, _____agree to follow the principles of digital citizenship outlined in this agreement and accept that failing to follow these tenets will have consequences.

Signed: _____

Name: _____ Date: ____ /____ /____

21st Century Fluency Project

Digital Citizenship Senior School Agreement

Respect Yourself

I will show respect for myself through my actions. I will select online names that are appropriate. I will consider the information and images I post online. I will not post personal information about my life, experiences, experimentation, or relationships. I will not be obscene.

Protect Yourself

I will ensure that the information I post online will not put me at risk. I will not publish my personal details, contact details or a schedule of my activities. I will report any attacks or inappropriate behavior directed at me. I will protect passwords, accounts and resources.

Respect Others

I will show respect to others. I will not use electronic mediums to flame, bully, harass, or stalk other people. I will show respect for other people in my choice of web sites. I will not visit sites that are degrading, pornographic, racist, or inappropriate. I will not abuse my rights of access and I will not enter other people's private spaces or areas.

Protect Others

I will protect others by reporting abuse, not forwarding inappropriate materials or communications, and not visiting sites that are degrading, pornographic, racist, or inappropriate.

Respect Intellectual Property

I will protect others by reporting abuse, not forwarding inappropriate materials or communications, and not visiting sites that are degrading, pornographic, racist, or inappropriate.

Protect Intellectual Property

I will request to use the software and media others produce. I will use free and open source alternatives rather than pirating software. I will purchase, license, and register all software. I will purchase my music and other media, and refrain from distributing these in a manner that violates their licenses. I will act with integrity.

By signing this agreement, I undertake to always act in a manner that is respectful to myself and others, and to act appropriately, and in a moral and ethical manner.

I, _____ agree to follow the principles of digital citizenship outlined in this agreement and accept that failing to follow these tenets will have consequences.

Signed: _____

Name: _____ Date: _____ / _____ / _____

Global Digital Citizenship Snapshot

To help you evaluate the level of proficiency that you or your students have with Global Digital Citizenship, use this tool. You can use it with individual students or with groups.

There are 10 statements below for you to consider. As you move through the statements, chose a value you feel represents the how well the individual or group you are evaluating has demonstrated the characteristic. Rate each statement from 1 (*strongly disagree*) to 5 (*strongly agree*). Better still, have your students assess themselves and discuss the outcome.

Move down the list, and then add up your total and multiply it by 2. This is the student's Global Digital Citizenship percentage, which you record in the box provided at the end of each list. From there, you can compare your results in each fluency to determine where focus and improvement may be needed.

global digital citizen

Personal Responsibility

Global Citizenship

Digital Citizenship

Altruistic Service

Environmental Stewardship

	1	2	3	4	5
I understand the importance of acting responsibly in digital and non-digital environments, and consistently act in such a manner.					
I know how to and consistently respect and protect myself and others, and act in an appropriate manner.					
I understand how to and consistently respect and protect intellectual property and self-published digital media (games, movies, images, software, etc.).					
I am willing to share my own intellectual property/resources and to help others discover their own creative potential.					
I give credit to and acknowledge references/authors/designers/co-workers where it is due and observe proper copyright laws and procedures.					
I understand the ideals and issues of other cultures and the environment, and respect others regardless of cultural or socio-economic differences.					
I am self-accountable and take personal responsibility for my actions and inactions related to our global and digital living and working environment.					
I consider short- and long-term effects of my actions on personal, environmental, and global levels, and practice diligence in preserving and maintaining each of these.					
I realize the importance of acting against racist, abusive, and inappropriate behavior and media, and cultivating altruism through charitable and compassionate acts.					
I adhere to a personal code of ethics based on global and digital citizenship, personal responsibility, altruistic service, and environmental stewardship.					

Global Digital Citizenship   %

global
digital citizen

Personal
Responsibility

Global Citizenship

Digital Citizenship

Altruistic Service

Environmental
Stewardship

Global Digital Citizenship Lesson Plan Grading Tool

The Lesson Plan Grading Tools are used to determine the degree of application of each of the 21st-century fluencies within the context of a unit plan. The Fluency Matrix is located on the front page of every unit plan. It is represented by a vertical line of colorful fluency icons that represent each of the 21st-century fluencies.

Below are a series of statements for you to consider that help to define the characteristics of Global Digital Citizenship within the context of a unit. Beside each statement is a 1 to 5 scale similar to the ones found in the Fluency Snapshot. As you work through each statement, consider the extent of its application in the unit, and rate each statement from 1 (*strongly disagree*) to 5 (*strongly agree*).

Move down the list, and then add your total up and multiply it by 2. This is the Global Digital Citizenship percentage, which is an estimation of how effectively a unit plan focuses on it's development in your students.

1 2 3 4 5

The challenge requires students to exercise ethical and respectful behavior when using digital media.

The challenge provides students with opportunities to take personal responsibility for their decisions and actions as both individuals and members of a collective.

The challenge/problem encourages students to demonstrate leadership and a sense of personal accountability.

The challenge promotes the importance and benefits of altruistic service to others.

The challenge demonstrates the importance of protecting and respecting themselves to students.

The challenge demonstrates the importance of respecting and protecting others to students.

The challenge demonstrates the importance of respecting and protecting intellectual property to students.

The challenge instills a sense of global responsibility by encouraging cross-cultural interactions, global research, or environmental considerations to be made.

The challenge is designed to make students aware of the importance of enacting and promoting appropriate Digital Citizenship ideals.

The challenge encourages students to reflect on past actions in both digital and non-digital environments, and think critically about future actions.

% Global Digital Citizenship

Summarizing the Main Points

- We have all become elevated to the status of global citizens, both socially and as a workforce. As such, we need to understand that we must be able to communicate and collaborate with people of other cultures, both in person and in virtual environments.

- Citizenship is no longer limited to the country in which one resides. Digital media has enabled communication, collaboration, dialogue, and debate on an international scale.

- Learning shifts from the teacher to the student.

- As global digital citizens, students need to be accountable for their learning.

- The basic 6 principles for a student's Digital Citizenship Contract should include:

  - Respect themselves.
  - Protect themselves.
  - Respect others.
  - Protect others.
  - Respect intellectual property.
  - Protect intellectual property.

Questions to Consider

- What does it mean to be a global digital citizen?

- What are the roles and responsibilities of a global digital citizen?

- How do the Internet and the rise of social media connect us in ways we could not have previously imagined?

- How do the roles and responsibilities of being a global digital citizen affect our decisions locally, nationally, and internationally?

- What would your Digital Citizenship Contract look like?

- How would you integrate altruistic service and environmental stewardship into your lessons to help your students become global digital citizens?

creating
relevance real-world

Chapter 10
The 21st-Century Learning Environment

> Education is what remains after one has forgotten everything he learned in school.
>
> Albert Einstein

Velcro Learning

There's an old saying you might've heard: "I hear and I forget. I see and I remember. I do and I understand." There is a lot of truth in this statement. In fact, there are decades of research telling us that what we are doing in education isn't working. Talking at and teaching at students is not effective. Only learning that has meaning sticks. Only teaching that is relevant to the learner is effective. This is called Velcro learning. A learner must be able to connect to what is being taught. Otherwise, the learning is like one side of Velcro: it just doesn't stick. Let's talk about what we know does work and how we can shift our instructional approach to create a 21st-century learning environment.

We know for certain that for students to remember and internalize information, they must move it from their short-term (working) memory to their permanent memory. For this to happen, four things are required.

1. Make It Sticky

The new information must connect to something the learner already knows and has already made meaning of. If the connection isn't there, the learner has to make one on the spot. Unless a connection is made, new content stays in working memory for only a few seconds. This is the difference between rote learning and meaningful learning.

Writer Eric Jensen says that we discard 98 percent of everything that comes into our brains. Have you ever been introduced to someone and instantly forgotten his or her name? Have you ever given your students a test on something and had them do really well, only to give them another test on the same material two weeks later and find it's as if they've never heard of the material before?

If the information is not meaningful to the learner, regardless of whether it's meaningful to the teacher, it will be quickly be discarded by the learner's brain. I want to restate that, because it is constantly forgotten by teachers: If the information is not meaningful, in other words relevant, to the learner, learning will not occur. It makes no difference if it's interesting, meaningful, or relevant to the teacher. It must be relevant to the student.

2. Draw From the Past

The second element is that new information must connect to previous knowledge and previous experiences. In other words, what students bring with them into the classroom determines not only what they'll learn but also if they'll learn.

3. Repeat, Repeat, Repeat

Learners have to be given differentiated learning opportunities that are repeatedly distributed over extended periods of time. If students don't understand something the first time around, you can't just walk up close and start talking to them more slowly and loudly and expect that method to work any better. Because learning doesn't usually stick the first time, students need multiple opportunities and a variety of experiences that provide both the time and the context for the ideas to be internalized.

4. Give Positive Feedback—Frequently

Students must be provided with consistent, positive feedback. They need to have their efforts reinforced regularly and meaningfully. According to a top video game developer, video games are designed so that game players are asked to make a critical decision about every one-half to one second and are positively reinforced or rewarded for those decisions every seven to 12 seconds.

In contrast, according to a recent research study, students on average receive positive reinforcement in the classroom only about once every 12 hours. Quality, formative feedback and positive reinforcement give learners what they need to better retain information. Students need to know that what they're doing is right, and then they need positive suggestions on how they can improve their performance.

If teachers do these four things consistently, research tells us, measurable learning will take place.

On a recent trip to Japan to visit his family, Lee took his 11-year-old niece, Anna, to the aquarium in her hometown. There was a huge shallow tank that all of the kids had their hands in. All over their hands were hundreds of garra rufa fish, also known as doctor fish.

These fish are found in river basins the Middle East and also live and breed in some outdoor pools in spas in Turkey. They feed on dead skin cells, and since they will only eat infected or dead areas, leaving the healthy skin to grow, they are used to help treat patients suffering from various skin disorders, such as psoriasis and eczema. Doctor fish spas have opened in Japan and dozens of countries around the world, including the United States.

Anna was curious about these fish, and the staff at the aquarium explained everything I've just told you. They also recounted that fact that Cleopatra used to bathe with doctor fish to keep her skin beautiful.

Suddenly, for Anna, a door was opened to inquire about geography, ancient Egypt, ancient Rome, and so much more. Why? Because these subjects are interesting to Lee? Because they're in the curriculum guide? No; because there was a real-world connection that brought relevance to the learning.

For learning to occur, there must be relevance, not to the teacher, but to the learner. So clearly the first component of the 21st-century learning environment is *relevance*.

Bloom's Digital Taxonomy and Higher-Order Thinking Skills

Bloom's Digital Taxonomy was developed by Andrew Churches and is the subject of an upcoming book. It is an update to Bloom's Revised Taxonomy, modified to take into account the new behaviors and learning opportunities emerging as technology advances and becomes more ubiquitous.

While Bloom's Taxonomy in its many forms does represent the learning process, it does not indicate that the learners must start at the bottom and work up. Learning can be initiated at any point, and the levels below will be encompassed within the scaffolded learning task.

Remember—Retrieving, recalling, or recognizing knowledge from memory; when memory is used to produce definitions, facts, or lists, or to recite or retrieve material.

Bloom's Digital Taxonomy

HOTS
creating
evaluating
analyzing
applying
understanding
remembering

| LOTS |

Key verbs: recognizing, listing, describing, identifying, retrieving, naming, locating, finding, bullet pointing, highlighting, bookmarking, social networking, social bookmarking, favoriting/local bookmarking, searching, googling

Understand—Constructing meaning from different types of functions, be they written or graphic.

Key verbs: exemplifying, advanced searches, Boolean searches, blog journalling, Twittering, categorizing and tagging, commenting, annotating, subscribing

Apply—Carrying out or using a procedure through executing or implementing; applying relates and refers to situations in which learned material is used through products such as models, presentations, interviews, and simulations.

Key verbs: implementing, carrying out, using, executing, running, loading, playing, operating, hacking, uploading, sharing, editing

Analyze—Breaking material or concepts into parts, determining how the parts relate or interrelate to one another or to an overall structure or purpose; mental actions include differentiating, organizing, and attributing as well as being able to distinguish between components.

Key verbs: comparing, organizing, deconstructing, attributing, outlining, structuring, integrating, mashing, linking, reverse engineering, cracking, media clipping, and mind mapping

Evaluate—Making judgements based on criteria and standards through checking and critiquing.

Key verbs: checking, hypothesizing, critiquing, experimenting, judging, testing, detecting, monitoring, (blog/vlog) commenting, reviewing, posting, moderating, collaborating, networking, reflecting, product (alpha and beta) testing, validating

Create—Putting the elements together to form a coherent or functional whole; reorganizing elements into a new pattern or structure through generating, planning, or producing.

Key verbs: designing, constructing, planning, inventing, devising, making, programming, filming, animating, blogging, video blogging, mixing, remixing, wiki-ing, publishing, videocasting, podcasting, directing/producing, building or compiling mashups

Obviously, we want to include the entire spectrum. If this is our goal, then a focus on creating will ensure the development of all the rungs of the taxonomy ladder. The second component of the 21st-century learning environment is creation.

Dale's Learning Cone

Edgar Dale first developed the learning cone in the 1960s. Over the years, his research has been reaffirmed again and again and adapted by people such as Glasser and Marzano. The actual percentages vary somewhat from study to study, and many people discount the information because of this. When looking at the learning cone, what is important is not the actual percentages but the fact that they are approximations representing a more substantial truth.

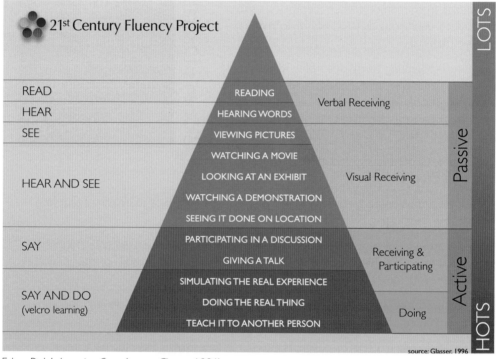

Edgar Dale's Learning Cone (source: Glasser, 1996)

According to the research, learners will remember less than 20 percent of the information they receive from reading or hearing after two weeks. This type of learning, which is a passive activity, is called *verbal receiving*.

The percentage of information retained jumps substantially for visual receiving, to as much as approximately 50 percent. Visual receiving, which involves combining two senses, includes activities such as watching a movie or seeing a demonstration. Both sight and hearing are involved, and this combination increases retention of information. Visual receiving, however, is still a passive activity.

We start to see significant retention when we move to active receiving. For example, participating in a discussion involves thinking about the information and forming an opinion or question. Comparing, contrasting, and evaluating are all necessary for participation, and overall higher-order thinking skills are used.

The most dramatic results come from simulating a real experience. Actually doing the real thing, or teaching it to another person, increases retention by as much as 90 percent. The information learned through this method sticks. In short, for learning to happen, as we have said before, there must be relevance in context for the learner.

Again, don't get hung up on the actual numbers. All the studies show that we remember very little of what we read and a whole lot of what we do. The argument that process- and problem-based learning takes too long just doesn't stand. In light of this research, which is more effective? Reading and lecturing or creating a real-world simulation?

Students are much more engaged when given the opportunity to do, to participate, and to create. Engagement means being involved or engaged in the process, and students need to be allowed to participate in and not be passive recipients of their education.

In every classroom and in every district where change is needed, teachers and students must make the shift. The switch to process- and problem-based learning can be uncomfortable at first, and it will take time to make this transition, but the payoffs outweigh the difficulties for both teacher and student.

Consider this: When students are engaged, there are fewer discipline problems. When students are allowed to create real-world products to demonstrate their understanding of the content, and the teacher is wise enough to pose problems and get out of the way to let the learning happen, those students amaze the teacher with what they're capable of doing. Teachers in turn are excited about coming to school every day, because they can't wait to see what they're going to learn from their students.

The third component of the 21st-century learning environment is *real world*.

In a 21st-century learning environment, students use higher-level thinking to create real-world products as solutions to relevant real-world problems.

Relevance

\+ Creating

\+ Real-world

─────────────────────

 21st Century Learning

Do you enjoy being lectured at all the time? When you were a student, did you enjoy having your teacher talk at you all the time?

Now in the same breath, let's be absolutely clear: there most certainly IS a time and place for telling—for full-frontal lecturing. It can be very useful when a lot of content has to be delivered quickly—we just can't do it all the time.

We need to shift our instruction from the traditional and predominantly full-frontal lecturing model to more of an emphasis on discovery learning. This method generates interest and therefore the relevance that is critical to learning.

Think about a scary action movie. Watching as the actors narrowly escape certain death and listening to the music creates a suspenseful atmosphere that keeps you on the edge of your seat as you wonder what's coming next. The experience is indelibly etched in your mind. But what if just before the movie began, someone told you what was going to happen, and that all of the actors make it through without a scratch? Or what if the people next to you talked to you throughout the movie, telling you what was going to happen next? It would rob you of the experience of finding these things out for yourself, because it would remove the elements of wonder and surprise. That's the problem created when we tell students what they need to know all or most of the time: It takes the excitement of discovery out of learning.

When students learn the material for themselves, it becomes their learning, not our teaching, and because it is their learning, they own it. They will remember it, they will be able to apply it, and they will be able to use it as the foundation for new learning and creating.

Instantly when we start talking about this, we hear the *yabuts*. "Yeah, but we don't have time." It's important to remember what we addressed when referring to Dale's learning cone and how much more information is remembered in a 21st-century learning environment for the time invested. "Yeah, but will they pass the mandated exam if I don't focus on content?" We're glad you asked.

Bertelsmann Study

A study that was conducted by the Bertelsmann Foundation in Michigan back in 1998 clearly demonstrates the effectiveness of cultivating higher-level thinking as well as measurable learning and retention. In the study, two groups of 100 social studies students were taught the same information by two different methods. One group was taught in the traditional way that's all too familiar to us: full-frontal lecturing with students sitting in rows. They poured over worksheets and were hammered with drills, drills, and more drills, and traditional tests and quizzes.

The second group learned primarily through problem- and process-based approaches. This group of students worked both individually and in groups. They benefited from self-assessment, peer assessment, and teacher assessment. They focused on creating real-world products to solve real-world problems.

At the end of the year, both groups were tested using the same traditional state-mandated exams for social studies. The results were stunning and most likely not what you would expect. The scores were nearly identical for both groups, regardless of how they learned.

You might be confused now as to the point of this. Perhaps you're thinking this indicates that there is no point in investing in technology or new instructional and assessment methods. Apparently the old approach still works just as well as ever.

You'd be wrong. One year later, unwarned and therefore unprepared, the students were given the very same test that the previous year they had passed with both groups performing equally well. The results were astonishing.

The group that was taught using traditional methods was able to recall only about 15 percent of the content. To make matters worse, an analysis of the results and the students' thinking indicated that they viewed social studies as a series of itemized facts—this happened on this date, this happened on that date, and one event did not influence another in any way. Theirs is an excellent example of lower-order thinking.

The group that was taught using problem- and process-based learning approaches recalled more than 70 percent of the content. More important, they demonstrated a deep understanding of the integrated nature of their learning. In other words, they not only remembered the content but also understood its significance. They were able to make abstract connections between events. Effective learners make attachments or connections between their existing knowledge and new information. This is Velcro learning! This is higher-order thinking. These are the goals we have for our students, and we need to make this shift in the instructional approach to give them the opportunity to develop the skills we know they need. They are limited not by their abilities but by our lack of flexibility in making the shift.

Stop Talking ... and Start Doing!

Even though this research has been around for decades, many educators continue to depend completely on the "stand and deliver; sit and learn" full-frontal lecture method. If we were to be really honest with ourselves, we know intuitively that this isn't working.

Teachers are good people who are committed to their students and want to do what's best for them. Yet what they're doing isn't working. They know this, but they continue to do it. Why? There is an unprecedented pressure on educators today. As our students are failing, fingers are being pointed at teachers. In many cases, teachers' salaries and employment are being tied to student performance.

Governments are demanding that more information be taught than there are hours available in the student's career. At the same time, millions of dollars are being slashed from budgets. In the panic to meet the mandates, teachers are attempting to cram as much information into students' heads as possible. Many students are seeing education as a 16-year process of slowly and painfully memorizing facts that can be Googled in seconds. The result is that they are tuning out and leaving school in unprecedented numbers—in some cases more than 50 percent of students. As we discussed earlier, this is happening not just in high schools but also in universities.

It's time to shift the instructional approach away from talking as teaching to problem- and process-based learning. In the 21st-century classroom, we must move the responsibility for learning from the teacher, where it traditionally has been, to the student, where it should be. Students must become active participants in their education. The teacher becomes the facilitator of learning, posing real-world problems that have relevance to the learners and guiding them through the process of creating a real-world solution. It's up to the students to decide how best to communicate their understanding. The learning is not scripted, and it doesn't limit students—they have the opportunity to explore, to communicate, and to create. While it is not an easy shift, it is very rewarding—for both teachers and students.

Setting the Scene

As the 21st-century learning environment revolves around real-world problems, teachers must transition to be crafters of these problems. A well-written scenario that connects real-world relevance to the learner, cultivates the 21st-century fluencies, and addresses curricular objectives sounds like a lot to ask for.

Like any skill, it takes time to develop. It also takes a willingness to make mistakes—that is what debriefing is all about—and finding a way to do it better next time.

In the next chapter, we walk you through the process of developing scenarios. We also provide samples and templates of the unit plans we have created for our 21st-Century Fluency Kits. This next chapter is the real meat of this book, so let's get at it and have some fun transforming your classroom into a 21st-century learning environment.

Summarizing the Main Points

- For students to remember and internalize information, they must move it from their short-term memory to their permanent memory.

- The first component of the 21st-century learning environment is relevance; not to the teacher, but to the learner. The second component is creation, which will ensure development of higher-order thinking. The third component is real world. In a 21st-century learning environment, students use higher-level thinking to create real-world products as solutions to relevant real-world problems.

- The responsibility for learning must be moved from the teacher to the student.

- Effective learners make connections between their existing knowledge and new information. This is called "Velcro learning."

Questions to Consider

- Consider Andrew Church's version of Bloom's Digital Taxonomy. How it is relevant to learners today?

- How can you incorporate process- and problem-based learning in your classroom?

- Why is the way we are teaching today not working, and what are the main reasons it must begin to change?

- In what ways has the role of the teacher changed in the 21st-century learning environment?

A President is Born
a 21st Century Fluency Project

language arts | grade **6**

10–12 periods

the big picture

Persuasive Speech, Politics, and Media

the essential question

What would be the important contributing factors that would give a running candidate the best chance of winning an election?

overview

Students will split into groups to each create a candidate for a fictional class president. They will create an original campaign poster and slogan, a compelling political speech, and will finally square off against each other in a mediated class debate centered around an issue in the news or affecting the local community.

curricular objectives

📖 **CC W.6.1.** Write arguments to support claims with clear reasons and relevant evidence.

📖 **CC W.6.5.** With some guidance and support from peers and adults, develop and strengthen writing as needed by planning, revising, editing, rewriting, or trying a new approach.

📖 **CC W.6.7.** Conduct short research projects to answer a question, drawing on several sources and refocusing the inquiry where appropriate.

📖 **CC SL.6.1.** Engage effectively in a range of collaborative discussions (one-on-one, in groups, and teacher led) with diverse partners on grade 6 topics, texts, and issues, building on others' ideas and expressing their own clearly.

📖 **CC SL.6.1.c.** Pose and respond to specific questions with elaboration and detail by making comments that contribute to the topic, text, or issue under discussion.

📖 **CC SL.6.5.** Include multimedia components (e.g., graphics, images, music, sound) and visual displays in presentations to clarify information.

solution fluency

information fluency

creativity fluency

media fluency

collaboration fluency

global digital citizen

core concepts matrix

📖🌱 political speech structure
📖🌱 presendential references
📖 persuasive writing
📖 persuasive speech

📖🅰 graphic design/layout
📖🌱 campaign strategies
📖🌱 debate skills/structure

* Language Arts 🅰 Math   Science 🌐 Social Studies

Chapter 11
21st-Century Fluency Lessons

> **Children have to be educated, but they also have to be left to educate themselves.**
>
> Ernest Dimnet, *The Art of Thinking*

In the 21st-century classroom, the instructional model shifts. The teacher is no longer the focal point of the classroom. Instead, students work in groups to create real-world solutions to real-world problems. Embedded within these problems are the curricular objectives. The teacher now takes on a new role as the facilitator of learning, presenting scenarios outlining real-world problems that are relevant to students and simultaneously aligned with curricular goals.

There are endless possibilities for crafting scenarios. At first, it may seem to be an overwhelming task, but rest assured that after you go through the process a few times, cultivating scenarios will become easier and you will be begin to see connections between the content that needs to be covered and everyday life experiences. One teacher shared this story with us:

> *I was standing in line at the coffee shop. I was looking around, mindlessly waiting for my turn, when I saw the barista take a paper cup off the big stack by the espresso machine. Instantly, this idea for a whole unit jumped into my head about sustainability. I started typing madly on my phone to try and capture some of the details.*
>
> *Suddenly I was at the counter with the huge line behind me. I asked the person taking my order to just hang on for a second while I finished my thought; then I let the person behind me go ahead. I realized it looked ridiculous. I looked like one of my students that I roll my eyes at. ,What's happened to me? I've turned into a thumbster teenager!*

Start With the Curriculum

Our entire educational system is built on standards. There is no getting away from the defined curriculum. Standards vary from state to state and country to country, but it makes no difference if your district has its own or aligns to the Common Core standards; you are still accountable for the curriculum. So the curriculum is an excellent place to start.

Select a single curricular objective. From that one objective, identify the specific skills or content that the students need to master. It is critical from the outset to remember that if we want to develop independent, lifelong learners, our intention must be to shift the burden of responsibility for learning from the teacher, where it has traditionally been, to the learner, where it truly belongs.

It is the students' job to learn the curriculum. The teacher's job is to guide them in that process, provide support, and develop a structure in which they can grow.

For learning to stick, it has to have relevance—not to the teacher, but to the learner.

What Would Be Relevant—in Context, or Applicable to Your Students' Lives?

The best place to start crafting a scenario is to ask yourself where your students may come across this information or this skill in their lives outside of school. If it's something they'll come across in their own world, then instantly there is a connection that brings relevance and context to the learner.

If nothing immediately comes to mind, try to identify the kinds of tasks that students would be performing when they applied these skills or used this knowledge, and consider how using this content could be made compelling for students.

At this point, many people start to think vocationally and consider professions that would involve this particular skill or knowledge. While that can be useful, this approach is often quickly discarded by students.

While we don't want teachers to discount situations in which people may predictably come across this type of challenge as part of their occupation, we should also work to identify occupations and skills that include unpredictable circumstances.

For example, if a nutritionist needs to use specific technical information related to a dietary matter and a student has no interest in becoming a nutritionist, the student will quickly disconnect from this information. In other words, there will be no personal relevance to the learner. Relevance must always be the top consideration in developing scenarios for learning to occur.

When using vocational examples, you have to ensure that there is relevance to the students. For example, what if a nutritionist was a consultant for your school's football team, helping the team members to fine-tune their healthy eating habits in hopes of helping them win the state championship? If your school is big on football, this might be something students could relate to. Better still, maybe this actually is a real-world example and the football team is involved. Perhaps the problem could be tied to specific players. Maybe the quarterback could provide a food journal of what he eats on a daily basis and the students could make recommendations as personal nutritionists. In this case, the quarterback might use the suggestions, gain 4 pounds of lean body mass, and drop his body fat by 3 percent. Maybe because of this, your school will win the state championship. All the students would then acknowledge you as one of the reasons for victory—your brilliant unit plan about nutritional strategies would have won them the championship. There would be a parade, and all the students would carry you on their shoulders shouting your name. A statue might be erected in your honor, and they would name the new football stadium after you.

All right, perhaps we're taking things a little too far, but do you see what we mean about connection? If students can relate to it, if they can get excited about it, and if they can connect to it, then they will learn from it, and this is easiest to do with a real-world scenario.

This can never be emphasized enough, so let's repeat it one more time. For learning to stick, it has to have relevance—not to the teacher, but to the learner.

Ripped From the Headlines

Once you're comfortable writing scenarios that are generic, you'll find yourself creating scenarios on the fly—just like the teacher who wrote to us about her coffee shop experience. You will start seeing possibilities everywhere, because they are everywhere!

The point of a good scenario, and therefore a good unit, is that it has relevance to the students—that it has real-world context. What better place to find real-world context than in the real world? Ask yourself what is happening in the world. How is what's happening going to affect us all? How can what is on the front page of the paper today be brought into the classroom?

You will find within newspaper and magazine stories the basis for dozens of scenarios. Every conceivable curricular objective for every subject—mathematics, social studies, language arts, economics, geography, science—it's all there! As an added bonus, if it's in the news, it's something your students can instantly relate to. When you find a connection between local, national, and global situations in a headline story, you have the makings of a great scenario.

How Can a Task Be Designed to Require Higher-Level Thinking?

Earlier, we discussed Bloom's Digital Taxonomy (refer back to chapter 10) and noted that lower-order thinking skills involve simply remembering or understanding. As we move up through applying, analyzing, evaluating, and finally creating, we cultivate higher-order thinking skills. If students are required to compare or contrast two or more things; if they are required to make inferences and find evidence to support generalizations; if they are required to form an opinion, or make a choice and justify the details with research; if they are asked to apply acquired knowledge, facts, techniques, and rules in a different way; if they are required to create something; or if they are asked to defend opinions by making informed decisions, then higher-level thinking is involved.

This, of course, is the objective. We want to ensure that by the time the students graduate, they are capable of unconsciously and consistently applying the higher-level skills of Bloom's Taxonomy in their everyday lives. For them to achieve this, students must be given repeated opportunities to practice these skills. This is why it's our responsibility to make sure higher-level thinking is involved in every educational scenario.

How Can Digital Tools Be Used to Create a Real-World Product That Demonstrates the Learning?

Wherever possible, the outcome should provide students with the opportunity to create, preferably with digital tools, a real-world product. Keep in mind the 6 Ds: Define, Discover, Dream, Design, Deliver, and Debrief. Delivery of a product must involve not only production but also publication. Publication is an essential step that allows students to debrief completely—to evaluate the product and the process through its real-world application to the original problem.

Putting It All Together

You now have everything you need to start assembling your scenario. This example is from a Grade 6 Language Arts lesson plan called "A President Is Born." In this lesson, students work in groups to develop unique class presidential candidates and design creative campaign packages for them. Later on, the candidates square off against each other in a structured class debate.

First, though, these are the Common Core State Standards we are addressing with this scenario:

CC W.6.1. Write arguments to support claims with clear reasons and relevant evidence.

CC W.6.5. With some guidance and support from peers and adults, develop and strengthen writing as needed by planning, revising, editing, rewriting, or trying a new approach.

CC W.6.7. Conduct short research projects to answer a question, drawing on several sources and refocusing the inquiry where appropriate.

CC SL.6.1. Engage effectively in a range of collaborative discussions (one-on-one, in groups, and teacher led) with diverse partners on grade 6 topics, texts, and issues, building on others' ideas and expressing their own clearly.

CC SL.6.1.c. Pose and respond to specific questions with elaboration and detail by making comments that contribute to the topic, text, or issue under discussion.

CC SL.6.5. Include multimedia components (e.g., graphics, images, music, sound) and visual displays in presentations to clarify information.

Create a Captivating Introduction

It's good to try provoking intrigue with a short, well-written introduction that is two or three sentences long. Here's an example:

> Our political leaders use various tools and strategies when running for an election. From a well-designed series of graphics to represent their ideas, values, and personalities, to a catchy and compelling campaign slogan to their crucial political speeches, candidates must do a great deal to promote themselves and their ideals.

This statement has a twofold purpose. First, it introduces the focus of the scenario. Anyone reading it will immediately get a sense of what the scenario is going to be about. Second, it introduces real-world flavor and concept. It generates the notion that the lesson will likely be relevant to real life. Find both of those concepts in your scenario and state them in your introduction if possible.

Introduce a Relevant Challenge

Next, you can introduce what the challenge is and how it involves students. At this point, it should be something that they will be interested in. Consider what topics, problems, or issues would engage them in an activity they would find challenging and fun. Our scenario continues with the following:

> Each group will dream up a running candidate for a fictional class president. Give the candidate a name, a unique personality, and a mission statement for the election. Your group will start by creating an original image for the candidate you are campaigning for, and there are no limitations here—person, animal, and so forth. Once you have created your running candidate, create a speech for him or her, which you will present orally.

> Next, create a unique and stand-out campaign poster for your candidate. It should be eye-catching, original, and define your candidate's personality and beliefs using images or maybe even a symbol of some kind. Also, make sure the poster includes a "campaign motto" or statement that is unique to your candidate.

See what we mean? Your challenges may vary, but the idea should have a real-world application and draw on student interest as well.

Give a Few Details to Pique Interest

It is important to not give too many details. Leave things out that students will have to discover as "purposely withheld information." However, the details you do want to provide should sum up the project in just a few short sentences. You should provide enough details to give students the idea that there will be required phases to the project without spelling out exactly what they'll be. We want to list only the things that are specific requirements while leaving as much room as possible for students to innovate a solution.

Once again, it's a quick but complete explanation of the intended components for the completed project. In other words, these sentences are what students are expected to produce and what teachers should be looking for in the final project.

> *Conduct research and gain insight by asking people about what kinds of work leaders and politicians do for the people they represent. Look at other leaders for inspiration and ideas. Revise and edit your speech as you gain new insight and knowledge through research, which must include human resources (e.g., parents, friends, community leaders, etc.). Your speech needs to be a compelling political speech.*

Sum It All Up in Define

Your written definition is a short description of what you are asking of your students when you develop the entire unit plan. It should be a quick summary that outlines the whole project. When you write your definition, it will help to ask yourself the question, "What is it that students have been asked to do in this scenario?" Read through the scenario, making notes of directives, and then summarize it in four or five sentences.

You must be able to pull out from the scenario a clear written definition of the problem. This is essential, because if you can't do it, then your students can't do it either. Consider this an opportunity to debrief and ask yourself how the scenario could be rewritten to be clear and concise but without scripting the outcome.

When we move to the unit plan, during the Define learning progression, the students will be required to provide a written definition of the problem. Your summary will be used as a comparison for formative assessment. It also will become instrumental in creating your assessment rubrics. The following is what the written definition for "A President is Born" would be.

> *Students have a clear understanding of their challenge for the lesson and have created a written definition that includes the tasks for the lesson. Each group will create a fictional class presidential candidate and a campaign slogan, speech, and poster for him or her. They will also participate as representatives for their candidate in a classroom debate on a chosen issue. They will provide persuasive arguments and solid points of view on the issue (what action they would take on it and why it is the best course of action).*

As an example, on the following page we present to you the entire scenario and written definition for "A President is Born." Use it as a reference point for ideas on how to word and structure when developing your scenario. Your own style will emerge quickly enough in your writing. Highlighted in bold are the points we have picked out as directives.

"A President Is Born": The Scenario

Our political leaders use various tools and strategies when running for an election. From a well-designed series of graphics to represent their ideas, values, and personalities to a catchy and compelling campaign slogan to their crucial political speeches, candidates must do a great deal to promote themselves and their ideals. In groups, take a look at the campaigns of recent political leaders and how they are structured to gain ideas for the next phase of the project. You can introduce videos or recordings of chosen campaign speeches for the class to consider and have them take notes as to what they observe about structure and content.

Each group will dream up a running candidate for a fictional class president. Give the candidate a name, a unique personality, and a mission statement for the election. Your group will start by creating an original image for the candidate you are campaigning for, and there are no limitations here—person, animal, and so forth. Once you have created your running candidate, create a speech for him or her, which you will present orally. Conduct research and gain insight by asking people about what kinds of work leaders and politicians do for the people they represent. Look at other leaders for inspiration and ideas. Revise and edit your speech as you gain new insight and knowledge through research, which must include human resources (e.g., parents, friends, community leaders, etc.). Your speech needs to be a compelling political speech.

Next, create a unique and stand-out campaign poster for your candidate. It should be eye-catching, original, and define your candidate's personality and beliefs using images or maybe even a symbol of some kind. Also, make sure the poster includes a "campaign motto" or statement that is unique to your candidate. It should be one short line that sums up your character's ideals and values and their pledge to the people if elected.

Finally, it's time to find out where your candidates stand on an important issue and how they would handle it if elected. With the teacher acting as mediator, the class will structure a debate about a chosen issue either in the news or in their community, and open a dialogue where the candidates square off and present their views and arguments. At the end of the debate, all groups will share their thoughts on how they felt each candidate represented himself or herself both on the campaign and in the issue debate and what strengths that candidate ultimately has as a vote-worthy figure.

The Acid Test for Scenario Development

Once you have developed a unit, you need to step back from it, do a Debrief, and find out how appropriate it is. Objectively, read your scenario and ask the following questions. If the answer to any of them is no, then go back to the beginning and review all of the steps until your scenario can pass this challenge.

- Is there a problem or challenge?
- Is this relevant to the learner?
- Does it require higher-level thinking?
- Does it address multiple curricular objectives?
- Does it cultivate the 21st-century fluencies?
- Are digital tools used to create a real-world product?
- Are there things that need to be discovered?

21st-Century Fluencies

Consider your scenario based on the chart below. If the scenario is properly crafted, the fluencies will be cultivated as a natural part of the learning process. You can use this chart below to easily evaluate this. The vertical axis is Bloom's Digital Taxonomy. It starts with lower-order thinking skills (LOTS) such as "remembering" at the bottom and moves progressively to higher-order thinking skills (HOTS) such as "creating" at the top.

The horizontal axis is Daggett's Application Model. Start with this, and ask yourself where your scenario fits into this model. Is it applicable in only a single unit, or can it be applied in a real-world, unpredictable situation?

Once you have determined this, ask yourself if the learner will pass the class with simply remembering or understanding only (LOTS) or if he or she is challenged with creating.

If your scenario is in the top right-hand corner of this chart, it is very effectively cultivating the vital 21st-century fluencies. If your scenario falls in the bottom left corner, you need to revisit the scenario development process and consider how to bring in higher-order thinking skills.

Creating Scenarios for 21st-Century Fluencies

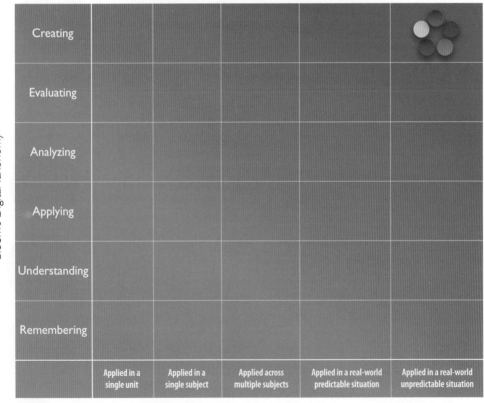

Bloom's Digital Taxonomy	Applied in a single unit	Applied in a single subject	Applied across multiple subjects	Applied in a real-world predictable situation	Applied in a real-world unpredictable situation
Creating					
Evaluating					
Analyzing					
Applying					
Understanding					
Remembering					

Adapted From Daggett's Application Model, 1998

A President is Born
a 21st Century Fluency Project

language arts · grade **6**
10–12 periods

overview
Students will split into groups to each create a candidate for a fictional class president. They will create an original campaign poster and slogan, a compelling political speech, and will finally square off against each other in a mediated class debate centered around an issue in the news or affecting the local community.

the essential question
What would be the important contributing factors that would give a running candidate the best chance of winning an election?

curricular objectives

- **CC W.6.1.** Write arguments to support claims with clear reasons and relevant evidence.

- **CC W.6.5.** With some guidance and support from peers and adults, develop and strengthen writing as needed by planning, revising, editing, rewriting, or trying a new approach.

- **CC W.6.7.** Conduct short research projects to answer a question, drawing on several sources and refocusing the inquiry where appropriate.

- **CC SL.6.1.** Engage effectively in a range of collaborative discussions (one-on-one, in groups, and teacher led) with diverse partners on grade 6 topics, texts, and issues, building on others' ideas and expressing their own clearly.

- **CC SL.6.1.c.** Pose and respond to specific questions with elaboration and detail by making comments that contribute to the topic, text, or issue under discussion.

- **CC SL.6.5.** Include multimedia components (e.g., graphics, images, music, sound) and visual displays in presentations to clarify information.

solution fluency

information fluency

creativity fluency

media fluency

collaboration fluency

global digital citizen

core concepts matrix

- political speech structure
- presendential references
- persuasive writing
- persuasive speech
- graphic design/layout
- campaign strategies
- debate skills/structure

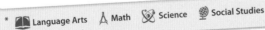

* Language Arts   Math   Science   Social Studies

The Components

The 21st-Century Fluency Kits Template is detailed but is nevertheless a straightforward lesson map. It is broken down into definitive sections. The first section is the Main Page. This page contains all the main technical, curricular information on the lesson plan at a glance. Here is an example of a Main Page with a complete breakdown:

Lesson Information: This includes the title, grade level, main core subject icon, and estimated class period duration of time.

The Big Picture: This is the main idea that drives the knowledge quest—it is often summed up in just one or two words.

Overview: This provides a brief description of the lesson plan's intended projects and outcome.

The Essential Question: This is the main question that is the focus of the lesson content derived from the Big Picture.

Core Subject Legend: Each core subject is represented by its unique icon. These icons appear in the subject balloon at the top, beside each standard, and in the Core Concept matrix.

Core Concepts Matrix: This indicates the learning concepts that are embedded throughout the lesson's content and activities. They come from multiple subject levels and help to provide a cross-curricular framework.

Curricular Objectives: These are the core standards covered by this lesson's content. One of the benefits of this type of learning is that it is practically impossible to limit the focus. By their very nature, students swell to address multiple curricular objectives—in the primary subject area and also in other subject areas.

Review your scenario at this point and compare it with the mandated curricular objectives. List all those that support it to some degree, and you'll find that there are lots of them. If students are to get the most value from a unit plan, it should obviously address as many curricular objectives as possible within the time allotted for the unit. Think about other curricular objectives and how your scenario can be modified to address these as well.

This is a great time to collaborate and to develop unit plans with members from other departments. Talk with your colleagues, discuss your ideas with them, and ask them for input on how your unit plans could be modified to address cross-curricular objectives and how their plans can be modified to address some of your concerns.

Fluency Matrix: This colored strand indicates the level of each 21st-century fluency that is exercised by this lesson's content, presented on a simple grading scale of 1 to 10. In each of the corresponding chapters, we provided the questions we use to arrive at the values assigned to each fluency.

As you can see, the Main Page contains the information you need to determine if your lesson plan will suit your specific instructional needs. The Curricular Objectives will give you an idea of the standards coverage provided by your lesson content. Equally useful is the addition of the Core Concepts Matrix, which allows you to see just how many concepts from varying core subjects are taught in this lesson plan. And, of course, consulting the Fluency Matrix will tell you how much of each vital 21st-century fluency skill is being cultivated.

A President is Born

Students will develop a political presidential figure for class president, a campaign poster and slogan, a running speech, and participate in a class debate on a predetermined topic.

High Tech: Students create a digital representation of their project's components, and film a campaign "commercial" using illustrations and video editing software.

Low Tech: Students use recording devices to record their candidate's speech as it may appear in a radio slot.

No Tech: Students design their candidate and poster using various art materials.

the scenario

Our political leaders use various strategies when running for an election. From a well-designed series of graphics to represent their ideals and personalities to a catchy and compelling campaign slogan, to their crucial political speeches, candidates must do a great deal to promote themselves and their ideals. Take a look at the campaigns of recent political leaders and how they are structured. You can introduce videos or recordings of chosen campaign speeches for the class to consider, and have them take notes as to what they observe about structure and content.

Each group in the class is going to dream up a running candidate for a fictional class president. Give your candidate a name, unique personality, and a mission statement for the election. Your group will start by creating an original image for the candidate you are campaigning for, and there are no limitations here—person, animal, etc. Create a speech for them, which you will present orally. Conduct research and gain insight by asking your parents and other people about what kinds of things leaders and politicians do to work for the people they represent. Look at other leaders for inspiration and ideas. Revise and edit your speech as you gain new insight and knowledge through research which must include human resources (parents, friends, community leaders etc). Your speech needs to be a compelling political speech. Next, create a unique and stand-out campaign poster for your candidate. It should be eye-catching and define your candidate's personality and beliefs using images or maybe even a symbol of some kind. Include a "campaign motto" or statement that is unique to your candidate. It should be one short line that sums up your character's ideals and values, and their pledge to the people if elected.

Finally, it's time to find out where your candidates stand on an important issue and how they would handle it if elected. With the teacher as mediator, structure a debate about a chosen issue either in the news or the community where the candidates square off and present their views and arguments. All groups will share their thoughts on how they felt each candidate represented themselves both on their campaign and in the issue debate, and what strengths that candidate ultimately has as a vote-worthy figure.

purposely withheld information

Students will need to examine the various components of a political campaign. Students will need to examine how political speeches are structured and written for effect. The students will also need to examine how political debates are conducted and mediated.

Setting the Scene

In this section, you are introduced to the technology-level applications of the lesson plan and options on how it can be used in learning environments that have varying degrees of access to digital tools. You will also be presented with the lesson's Scenario—the main story on which the lesson is centered, which reveals the specific challenges and guidelines the students are required to follow while engaged in their lesson projects.

In addition to this, we cover Purposely Withheld Information and the questions you can ask to alter or expand the challenge focus of your lesson plan, giving you the freedom to vary its outcomes and purposes for the learner.

Tech-Level Applications: In this section, we offer options for how the unit can be implemented in high-, low-, and no-tech environments. Your decisions will be based primarily on what technology is readily available in the teaching environment. You will find that your students have lots of different suggestions on how they can complete the project. Be open to their ideas; your students' suggestions mean they are engaged.

The Scenario: This is the lesson plan story. The scene is described, the challenge is issued, and the requirements for producing a solution to the problem are detailed. The scenario follows a general strand of ideas that describes everything that should have been accomplished by the students when the lesson is over.

Purposely Withheld Information: In every lesson, there are things students must discover for themselves in their journey. These concepts, which are detailed in this section, are the ones the students must uncover and use in their projects through research and by going on a quest for information that they can incorporate into their challenge solutions. This section is included to remind us what not to tell our students.

When a student asks a question in a problem- and process-based classroom, the answer from the teacher generally should be something like this: "Hey, that's a really good question! What do you think the answer is? Where do you think you can find out? Does anyone else have that question? Maybe you can work together to discover the answer."

Obviously, this is an oversimplification. There are questions that we have to answer for our students. For the most part, we have to remember that this is their learning and it's their responsibility. The teacher is the easiest source for answers, but when students graduate, their teachers will no longer be there to support them. How will they get the answers they need then? This is the mindset that you need to have when you transition your class to problem- and process-based learning. Our job is not to show the students how smart we teachers are but to help them discover how intelligent they can be in solving problems for themselves. When students graduate from our schools, they shouldn't need us any more. They need to become independent and flexible thinkers who can solve real-world problems by themselves.

If we are going to wean our students from this culture of dependency on the teacher, we must provide them with incomplete information. Consider what material you should withhold from your students because you want them to discover it for themselves. If part of the hidden objective of a unit is for your students to discover what causes an earthquake, then that's an example of the type of information you don't want to provide them.

Next, we'll begin to take a look at the steps involved in putting the lesson content to work inside your classroom.

the learning process

1–2 periods

exploring learner assumptions

The students will receive the Big Picture and consider the Essential Question. Lead them in a discussion of their views and any notions they might have on addressing the question of how to organize and run a successful political campaign.

1–2 periods

define

In this lesson, student groups will create a fictional class presidential candidate and create a campaign slogan, speech, and poster for him or her. They are required to participate as reps for their candidate in a classroom debate on a chosen issue. They must provide persuasive arguments and solid points of view on the issue and what action they would take on it, and why it is the best course of action. In this respect, they are also encouraged to challenge the other candidates' viewpoints.

Prerequisites for Progression

Students have produced a clear idea of the task of creating a candidate for class president and incorporating the components of a successful campaign and have successfully created a written definition including: Create a character to participate in a fictional class president election, including name, personality and mission for the election and icon. Research what work leaders do to represent their voters and how they do it. Include human resources in the research. Develop a compelling political speech. Create a campaign poster that reflects the beliefs and personality of the candidate. The poster must include a slogan and images or graphics. Participate in a debate, representing the candidates views.

1–2 periods

discover

In this stage, students get a chance to examine the makings of good political campaigns. Each group can examine recent elections and look into the campaigns designed by the individuals running. They should examine the steps involved and who is responsible for what job in the procedure. They should examine the structure of components like successful campaign speeches, campaign slogans, logo and poster designs, and the attributes that make all these things unique. They should look at how all these things are related to one another, and how they incorporate and represent the values and specific personality of the candidate they're designed for.

Prerequisites for Progression

Students have completed their examination and research and interviews on political campaign components and techniques for building their effectiveness, making a record of what they discover for reference as the project moves forward.

The Learning Process

Since the focus in the 21st-century classroom is problem solving, we use Solution Fluency as the learning progressions. This allows students to internalize this structured problem-solving process. Let's go through all these steps in a little more detail just as they appear in the lesson plan template pages.

Exploration of Learner Assumptions

In this stage, we present the Big Picture and Essential Question and facilitate a discussion with the students. We are looking for them to verbalize what they know and what their assumptions are about these questions. The goal is to guide the discussion from what they feel they are already knowledgeable about or familiar with concerning the subject through to opinion and speculation. The idea is for them to speak openly and share ideas about the issues brought up in the Essential Question. You can also provide a list of questions or ideas on how to facilitate and expand this discussion. A good facilitation will generate a lot of interest in the topic because students become personally involved—their thinking and opinions are being challenged and they have a vested interest in the subject.

Define

With the engagement level high, the scenario is then presented and teams are assigned if appropriate. It is at this point that the students are made aware of the guidelines for the lesson. Once experienced with the process, they will know that they must pay careful attention to the scenario because it contains the task. The individuals or teams then work on defining the problem and creating a clear and accurate written definition.

Prerequisites for Progression: Each learning progression becomes a natural point at which to provide formative feedback. Breaking the learning progressions down into manageable pieces that are in fact the stages of Solution Fluency allows you to guide your students throughout the entire process, helping to keep them aligned with the intended outcome.

At this first checkpoint, the students illustrate their understanding of the problem or challenge they must face, along with an understanding of the requirements for their project. In the scenario development section (pages 104–105), a written definition was produced as part of the process of evaluating the scenario. That statement belongs here, to describe what the students must complete so that they can proceed. In the Define stage's Prerequisite for Progression, the students must be able to create a written definition of the problem presented to them and of the tasks they will be required to perform. Use it to compare the essential elements of the project against the definition the students develop, guiding them to revise their definition if necessary.

Discover

Discover is the process of investigation, looking backward in time to determine how a problem developed. It explains what could have been done differently in the past that would've provided a different outcome and how similar problems have been solved in the past. Discovery also includes gathering relevant information to assist in gaining context and understanding of the problem. Your directions in this section of the lesson plan will include how to guide your students in the Discover process and suggestions to help direct them in the knowledge quest, which will also include appropriate research into the subject matter.

Prerequisites for Progression: To proceed, students must have collected a body of research on the subject matter and familiarized themselves with the content to begin the next phases. They will incorporate this new knowledge extensively into the next steps. List the requirements based on your scenario and expectations for a thorough investigation here.

A President is Born

the learning process

dream

Let students ponder what they've learned and continue making discoveries as they think about what they want their fictional class presidential running candidate to look like, act like, and represent. Guide them towards thinking about a unique look and personality development for their candidate. They should also consider what their candidate stands for, what they value and are passionate about, and what they would like to achieve for their class, its students, and perhaps the entire school. Ensure the students try their best to determine what is important to the students in a bid to give their candidate and campaign relevance and staying power. They will also need a clear set of values that will support their arguments in the upcoming class debate.

Prerequisites for Progression

Students have a clear visualization of the candidate design and profile, and a preliminary outline of how they will design their campaign components.

design

In this stage, students can now begin fleshing out their ideas for candidate design, campaign posters, slogans, logos, and a compelling political speech. You could get them to consult other parties such as parents, friends, or even some local successful political figures to determine what the proper strategies are in campaign and speech development.

Prerequisites for Progression

Students have created outlines for their candidate and their personality profile, poster ideas, an original campaign slogan and logo, and an outline for the candidate's running speech, and a plan for completing the development of the project.

deliver—produce

All outlines and ideas are now revised, edited, finalized, and presented. Posters and other graphics can be hung up around the classroom or school, and the project can be expanded into an informal vote in which other students weigh in on which candidates they may likely vote for in an election. Groups can also deliver their campaign speeches. This is also a good time to announce the topic for the candidate's debate.

Prerequisites for Progression

Students have created their candidate and poster/logo/slogan ideas, and have placed the posters in plain view for consideration and critique. They have also presented their candidate's campaign speech. They have also been made aware of the topic for the ensuing candidate's debate.

Dream

With the newly discovered context, students have a solid foundation to consider a solution. The Dream stage includes brainstorming to develop a SMART solution, meaning that it is specific, measurable, attainable, realistic, and timely.

This section provides directions on how to guide this process for students. It is about generating a visualization of how the best SMART solution would look using the parameters in the lesson scenario and the Define stage. This is the place for students to let their creative imaginations soar as they conceptualize their solutions.

Prerequisites for Progression: Students will provide a written explanation of the intended solution demonstrating an understanding of the purpose of the message, who the target audience is, and consideration for the time and resources available as well as the skill level of the team. They will then "pitch" the concept to the teacher, who can help them evaluate the concept.

Design

This stage involves mapping of the production process for the project, creating a timeline with specific milestones, deadlines, and responsibilities. In this area belong details and directions about how to manage the process. For example, if one of the intended solutions is a slide presentation, a resource outlining the various phases normally associated with completing that type of project would be included. This becomes a baseline for assessing the proposed design submissions of the students.

Prerequisites for Progression: This will depend on the various solution designs that your students generate, but this set of prerequisites generally involves submitting a realistic completed timeline with specific milestones, deadlines, and responsibilities assigned to each team member.

Deliver—Produce

In the production phase, the delivery method or product that is being created will determine the content of this phase. It may be that several phases need to be added here, depending on the complexity of the project. For example, properly developing a media project involves preproduction, production, and postproduction, each with its own set of criteria. At the end of the production phase, however, the students' products will be completed and ready to publish or present.

Prerequisites for Progression: This phase sees the students' completed products, as defined in the Dream phase. The projects must have followed all the preset guidelines, and they must include all necessary components if there are multiple requirements. This will indicate that your students are ready to move on to the second part of the Deliver phase.

the learning process

deliver—publish

Each group now has a chance to square off and challenge each other in a debate on a chosen topic. The topic can be local, school-oriented, or wider in scope such as territorial or even global. Each representative weighs in and discusses the topic with teacher as mediator for the debate. Here are some questions to get the ball rolling:

- Why is this a relevant issue to the students/community?
- What will happen if the issue is left unchecked?
- What would your candidate personally do to help this situation?
- What would be the potential drawbacks of a course of action?
- What is your candidate's personal pledge to address this problem if elected?

Prerequisites for Progression

Student groups have introduced their candidate and completed delivery of their campaign speeches. They have also participated as active representatives of their candidate in a teacher-mediated class debate on a pre-chosen topic.

debrief

All the groups can now discuss as a class what they thought of each individual group's campaign development. What did they like, and what could have been improved? Was it a potentially compelling candidate and campaign? If so, what made it that way? Urge them to reflect and discuss what they've learned about the work involved in a political campaign design, and what makes them successful and stand out above others.

Deliver—Publish

The second half of Deliver is publishing. When discussing Solution Fluency, we mentioned that it is not enough to create a presentation; you have to give the presentation. This is truly delivering the solution. In the Publish phase, groups of students may give their presentations to other groups. If so, an excellent strategy is to use peer assessment as well as self-assessment for evaluation and to encourage questions from the other groups for clarification.

This section also will provide some sample questions for you to ask that would demonstrate a higher level of understanding of the problem, depending on how well the research was done and students' attained knowledge of the subject. This section will also provide suggestions for criteria to use when critiquing the product presentation. You're also encouraged to think of your own questions and criteria to make the most of this stage in the lesson.

Prerequisites for Progression: To progress to the final stage, students will have completed the publishing phase in accordance with the project specifications. Any assessments that were required must also be completed.

Debrief

The final stage of the learning progressions is the Debrief. This often overlooked stage is critical in the lesson plan and is often quite revealing for the students. Having completed an entire learning journey, they now have the opportunity to look back and see what was learned.

Debriefing involves analyzing how the product and process could have been made better. If time permits, students may make adjustments to improve the project. Regardless, an understanding of how to improve the product and the process next time will help students to become better with Solution Fluency.

In addition, this phase should include a group discussion revisiting the initial assumptions, providing everyone with the opportunity to see measurable learning progress and the value of the time invested in it.

A President is Born

4

The group created a unique and interesting presidential candidate with strong personality traits and an excellent set of clearly-defined ideas and values. Their poster, slogan, and logo designs are very effective at profiling/representing the candidate. The posters were very eyecatching and composed creatively. All the campaign components related well and complimented each other. A compelling and inspiring speech was written and presented for this particular candidate. Representatives participated actively in the class debate and presented well-formed ideas and strong, logical viewpoints and arguments.

3

The group has created an interesting presidential candidate with some good personality traits and a well-defined set of ideas and values. Their poster, slogan, and logo designs were effective at profiling/representing the candidate. The posters are eyecatching and composed creatively. All the campaign components related well and complimented each other. A compelling and inspiring speech was written and presented for this particular candidate. Representatives actively participated in the class debate and presented mostly well-formed ideas and logical viewpoints and arguments.

2

The group created a presidential candidate with some good personality traits and a loosely-defined set of ideas and values. Their poster, slogan, and logo designs showed some creativity. Most of the campaign components related and complimented each other, but others did not. A speech was written and presented for this particular candidate. Representatives participated in the class debate to a limited degree, and struggled to present good ideas, viewpoints, and arguments.

1

The group created an uninteresting presidential candidate who lacked personality and a clear set of ideas and values. Their poster, slogan, and logo designs were not particularly effective at profiling/representing the candidate, and weren't eyecatching or creative. All the campaign components seemed random, unrelated, and struggled to compliment each other. The speech that was written and presented for this particular candidate was lackluster, uninteresting, and uninspiring. The representatives were not very active in the class debate, and when they did participate were unable to present good ideas, viewpoints, and arguments.

Rubrics

Before we discuss rubrics, we'd like to make an important point. The process of evaluation is often hidden from students, and it shouldn't be. Every rubric should be produced in a way that would allow the students to use it and evaluate their own work or the work of their peers. In fact, we believe strongly that students should always be involved in the assessment process, and we suggest you consider providing them with the Project Rubric at the beginning of the project—it clearly identifies what they must accomplish.

In creating our unit plans, we developed four rubrics. They provide a starting point and are designed to assist in evaluating the project and also your students' progress in gaining an understanding of the curricular objectives. You may find it necessary to develop additional rubrics when customizing the unit for use in your classroom.

Project Rubric

The first of our three rubrics is the Project Rubric. It is developed from our original Define paragraph developed when creating the scenario. This rubric is designed to evaluate specifically what we have asked of the students. For example, if we asked them to create a 10-minute presentation that communicates who Paul Revere was, when he lived, and what his significance was in American history, these will be the primary points represented in the rubric.

This rubric is well suited for self-assessment and peer assessment, as it is a summation of the project. Using this rubric with your students will give them the opportunity to understand evaluation and make the connection between the problem and the expected outcome. This will serve to help them become better problem solvers.

Let's go a little deeper into how these rubrics are developed for student evaluation. The first thing we ask is, what specifically have the students been tasked with? If they have understood the problem clearly and been able to demonstrate that in the Define phase, they should expect full marks if they meet all the criteria. So we start with "What have they been asked to do?" Here is the challenge from "A President is Born." In bold are the points that become our definition.

> *Our political leaders use various tools and strategies when running for an election. From a well-designed series of graphics to represent their ideas, values, and personalities to a catchy and compelling campaign slogan to their crucial political speeches, candidates must do a great deal to promote themselves and their ideals. In groups, take a look at the campaigns of recent political leaders and how they are structured to gain ideas for the next phase of the project. You can introduce videos or recordings of chosen campaign speeches for the class to consider and have them take notes as to what they observe about structure and content.*

> ***Each group will dream up a running candidate for a fictional class president. Give the candidate a name, a unique personality, and a mission statement for the election.*** *Your group will start by* ***creating an original image for the candidate*** *you are campaigning for, and there are no limitations here—person, animal, and so forth. Once you have created your running candidate,* ***create a speech for him or her, which you will present orally.***

> *Conduct research and gain insight by asking people about what kinds of work leaders and politicians do for the people they represent. Look at other leaders for inspiration and ideas. Revise and edit your speech as you gain new insight and knowledge through research, which must include human resources (e.g., parents, friends, community leaders, etc.). Your speech needs to be a compelling political speech.*

A President is Born

learning process formative rubric

define

above

Students have produced a clear idea of the task of creating a candidate for class president and incorporating the components of a successful campaign and have successfully created a written definition including: Create a character to participate in a fictional class president election, including name, personality and mission for the election and icon. Research what work leaders do to represent their voters and how they do it. Include human resources in the research. Develop a compelling political speech. Create a campaign poster that reflects the beliefs and personality of the candidate. The poster must include a slogan and images or graphics. Participate in a debate, representing the candidates views.

below

discover

above

Students have completed their examination and research and interviews on political campaign components and techniques for building their effectiveness, making a record of what they discover for reference as the project moves forward.

below

dream

above

Students have a clear visualization of the candidate design and profile, and a preliminary outline of how they will design their campaign components.

below

*Next, **create a unique and stand-out campaign poster for your candidate. It should be eye-catching, original, and define your candidate's personality and beliefs using images or maybe even a symbol of some kind.** Also, **make sure the poster includes a "campaign motto" or statement that is unique to your candidate.** It should be one short line that sums up your character's ideals and values and their pledge to the people if elected.*

*Finally, it's time to find out where your candidates stand on an important issue and how they would handle it if elected. With the teacher acting as mediator, **the class will structure a debate about a chosen issue either in the news or in their community, and open a dialogue where the candidates square off and present their views and arguments.** At the end of the debate, all groups will share their thoughts on how they felt each candidate represented himself or herself both on the campaign and in the issue debate and what strengths that candidate ultimately has as a vote-worthy figure.*

Let's break this scenario down into point form:

- Dream up a candidate for class president, including name, unique personality, and missions statement.
- Create a speech that will be presented orally.
- Create a unique, eye-catching, and original campaign poster that represents your candidate's personality and beliefs. Use images, and include a unique campaign motto.
- Participate in a debate presenting the views and arguments of your candidate.

Note that if we take the time to do this, we have exactly what we need for the prerequisite for progression in the Define phase. In fact, this is how we came up with our written definition earlier. Here it is again to compare against our points above:

Students have a clear understanding of their challenge for the lesson and have created a written definition that includes the following: Create a fictional class presidential candidate and a campaign slogan, speech, and poster for him or her. Participate as representatives for their candidate in a classroom debate on a chosen issue. Provide persuasive arguments and solid points of view on the issue (what action they would take on it and why it is the best course of action).

Now we begin with Level 2—Acceptable. This is a summation of the bare minimum that was asked for in the project. In the 21st-century learning environment, students are expected to excel, to go above and beyond, and this is reflected in the rubrics. There is ample room for them do better than what is expected. We also need to evaluate the quality of their efforts. Here are a few sentences that evaluate the presentation and then our criteria, worded in past tense with a value comparison of the criteria:

The group has created a rather ordinary presidential candidate with a few noticeable personality traits and a set of loosely defined ideas and values.

Their poster, slogan, and logo designs are somewhat effective in both profiling the candidate and representing his or her political mission and values. Their poster is basic and has some creativity.

A somewhat effective speech was written and presented for this particular candidate.

Representatives participated in the class debate to a limited degree and struggled to present their ideas, viewpoints, and arguments.

A President is Born

curricular objectives rubric

above

CC W.6.1. Write arguments to support claims with clear reasons and relevant evidence.

below

above

CC W.6.5. With some guidance and support from peers and adults, develop and strengthen writing as needed by planning, revising, editing, rewriting, or trying a new approach.

below

above

CC W.6.7. Conduct short research projects to answer a question, drawing on several sources and refocusing the inquiry where appropriate.

below

above

CC SL.6.1. Engage effectively in a range of collaborative discussions (one-on-one, in groups, and teacher led) with diverse partners on grade 6 topics, texts, and issues, building on others' ideas and expressing their own clearly.

below

Now that we have our Level 2 definition, we copy it and rework the language for the value comparison representing Level 3—Very Good. Compare these two levels and note that we are accomplishing this by changing only a few words, which are highlighted in bold.

*The group has created **an interesting** presidential candidate with **some** personality traits and a set of **clearly-defined** ideas and values.*

*Their poster, slogan, and logo designs are **mostly** effective in both profiling the candidate and representing his or her political mission and values. Their poster is **fairly** eye-catching **and** creative.*

*An **effective** speech was written and presented for this particular candidate.*

*Representatives **participated** in the class debate and **presented** their ideas, viewpoints, and arguments **well**.*

Next we consider Level 4—Excellent. This is the highest level of the rubric. We start here because we need to detail what excellence is, and this will vary greatly. What is excellent for a student in Grade 6 would most likely not be excellent for a student in Grade 12. As a teacher, you know what your students are capable of and can outline what is achievable for them. They will only reach this level if they go above and beyond the requirements or do an exceptional job.

*The group has created a **unique** and interesting presidential candidate with **charismatic** personality traits and a set of clearly defined ideas and values.*

*Their poster, slogan, and logo designs **are effective** in both profiling the candidate and representing his or her political mission and values. Their poster **is eye-catching** and creative.*

*A **compelling** and inspiring speech was written and presented for this particular candidate.*

*Representatives participated **actively** in the class debate and presented **well-formed** ideas and **strong, logical** viewpoints and arguments.*

If the team members did not complete the project, they will obviously get a 0. Otherwise, they will end up with Level 1—Unacceptable. In the final stage of rubric development, we take our text from Level 2 and reduce the value comparisons down to what would be considered unacceptable when considering our original definition of the problem.

*The group has created **an uninteresting** presidential candidate with **no real** personality traits **or any** defined ideas and values.*

*Their poster, slogan, and logo designs **are ineffective** in both profiling the candidate and representing his or her political mission and values. Their poster **is not very** eye-catching or creative.*

*An effective speech **was not** written and presented for this particular candidate.*

*Representatives **seldom** participated in the class debate and **did not** present their ideas, viewpoints, and arguments well when they did.*

On page 118 is the completed rubric as it is presented to the students to use. For some projects, depending on duration and complexity, it's all that will be required. In fact, oftentimes this is the only rubric that is needed.

components rubric

4	3	2	1
presidentail candidate development			
Unique and interesting, strong personality traits, excellent set of clearly-defined ideas and values.	Interesting, good personality traits and a good set of clearly-defined ideas and values.	Some good personality traits and a loosely-defined set of ideas and values.	Lacked personality and a clear set of ideas and values.
design components			
Designs are very effective at profiling the candidate; eyecatching and composed creatively.	Designs are effective at profiling the candidate; eyecatching and composed creatively.	Designs are mostly effective at profiling the candidate; are somewhat creative.	Designs are not effective at profiling, the candidate; weren't eyecatching or creative.
design consistency and relation			
All the campaign components related well and complimented each other.	Most campaign components related well and complimented each other.	Some campaign components related well and complimented each other.	Campaign components did not relate well or compliment each other.
presidential speech			
A compelling and inspiring speech was written and presented for this candidate.	An inspiring speech was written and presented for this candidate.	A basic speech was written and presented for this candidate.	An uninteresting speech was written and presented for this candidate.
class debate participation			
Participated actively and presented good ideas and strong, logical viewpoints.	Participated and presented mostly good ideas and some logical viewpoints.	Participated to a limited degree, struggled to present ideas and logical viewpoints.	Did not actively participate, and were unable to present logical ideas and viewpoints.

Project Components Rubric

The previous rubric is useful, but what if the group does a fabulous job on most parts of the project but fails in one area? The result might be a Level 1 evaluation, though the balance of the project was at Level 4. To prevent this, we also use a components rubric. It, like all rubrics, can be used for self- and peer assessment as well. Constructing this rubric becomes very easy if we have built the previous one in the manner we suggested, by starting with a written Level 4 and then duplicating the text for the other levels and modifying the language.

The Components Rubric is built using the related sentences from the Projects Rubric, broken down by concept. It's easiest to explain by example. The image on page 122 is the Components Rubric for the "A President is Born" project.

Learning Process Formative Rubric

Each of the learning progressions in our unit plans has a prerequisite for progression—a list of what the student must accomplish in order to proceed to the next step in the process. The text from those areas is duplicated in this rubric and can then be used with students to guide their progress with formative feedback, which is in essence a mini-debrief, helping them to refine their processes and product at critical points throughout their development. It is particularly helpful if the prerequisites for progression are written in a past-tense rubric style that students can understand clearly. A sample of the Learning Process Formative Rubric is on page 118.

Common Core Rubrics

The aim of the 21st-century classroom is to cultivate the 21st-century fluencies while still addressing the mandated curricular objectives. The units we produce for publication in our 21st-Century Fluency Kits align with Common Core Standards for mathematics and English language arts and McRel Standards for areas not yet covered by the Common Core. Your district may also use the Common Core or perhaps have additional standards as well. Whichever standards you use to build your scenarios, these are the ones for which you are accountable and with which your students are expected to become proficient.

Most standards are not addressed completely in any one unit and then forgotten. Instead, they will appear in many units and be cultivated over time. We use the Common Core Rubric to provide formative feedback to the students so that they will understand what the standards are and how they are performing and progressing.

Similar to the design of the Learning Process Formative Rubric, each standard is listed along with space for formative feedback explaining to the students why they are above or below the standard.

We provide two Common Core rubrics—one for the primary subject area and a second for standards from secondary subject areas that are applicable in the particular unit.

Earlier we listed the Common Core Standards we are addressing in the unit "A President is Born." The Common Core Rubric can be found on page 120.

questions and ideas to expand this unit

cultivating global digital citizenship

- Turn your class into a special corporation or organization aimed at promoting good citizenship and peer support to all other students.

- Work with local community leaders to organize environmental clean-up campaigns and encourage other schools to join.

- Create podcasts and spotlight documentaries on runnings for class presidents or special club or activity leaders to teach the elements of good behaviour in campaigns using digital networking platforms.

* Personal Responsibility   Global Citizenship   Digital Citizenship   Altruistic Service   Environmental Stewardship

Why are political leaders important to the structure of an organized society?

McREL Civics—Standard 3.—Level III—1. Understands the difference between the "rule of law" and the "rule of men" (e.g., government decisions and actions made according to established laws vs. arbitrary action or decree).

What are the responsibilities of various classes of political leader or decision-makers?

McREL Civics—Standard 5.—Level III—1. Understands the primary responsibilities of each branch of government in a system of shared powers (e.g., legislative, executive, judicial) and ways in which each branch shares the powers and functions of the other branches.

What would be the short and long-term effects of a society without socio-political structure?

McREL Civics—Standard 1.—Level III—4. Understands major ideas about why government is necessary (e.g., people's lives, liberty, and property would be insecure without government; individuals by themselves cannot do many of the things they can do collectively such as create a highway system, provide armed forces for the security of the nation, or make and enforce laws).

2. Understands how and why the rule of law can be used to restrict the actions of private citizens and government officials.

3. Understands the possible consequences of the absence of a rule of law (e.g., anarchy, arbitrary and capricious rule, absence of predictability, disregard for established and fair procedures)

How are bills passed and made into law?

McREL Civics—Standard 4.—Level III—4. Knows some basic uses of constitutions (e.g., to set forth the purposes of government, to describe the way a government is organized and how power is allocated, to define the relationship between a people and their government)

The Resources Page

Following the rubric is a comprehensive list of information tools that can be utilized throughout the various stages of the learning progressions. These include useful resources that apply to different stages or even to learning concepts that appeared in the Core Concepts Matrix on the Main Page. This page has resources that are suitable for both teacher and learner.

Cultivate Global Digital Citizenship

The criteria that define the ideal global digital citizen can be broken down into five distinct categories—personal responsibility, global citizenship, digital citizenship, altruistic service, and environmental stewardship. In chapter 9, we explained each of these characteristics in detail. This section of the unit plan provides suggestions for activities within the unit or extensions of the unit that cultivate each of these characteristics.

Concepts and Questions for Expansion

Following the suggestions for global digital citizenship are ideas for additional projects and questions that can be asked within the unit for your consideration. These are offered as some suggestions to move the lesson plan in other directions. You can use these ideas to challenge and nurture different skill sets and abilities in your students and lead them on other fun and fulfilling problem-solving quests. Asking the right questions is what leads students on the quest for information, and it is part of the process used in Information Fluency. Each question or idea is followed by a partial list of the additional curricular objectives that would be added by its inclusion in the unit.

Unit Plan Template

On our web site (http://www.fluency21.com), you can access our online unit-planning tool, which you can use to develop and archive your ideas as well as share them with others. The following is a paper-based version to help you sketch out your units. A PDF copy of this file is available in the resources section of our web site.

Sample Unit Plans

At the end of this book are some completed sample unit plans from different grades and subjects to give you an idea of what is possible. Complete 21st-Century Fluency Kits are being developed that include a book of units specific to each grade and subject area along with substantial resources. We hope these will inspire and assist you in developing your own units.

Summarizing the Main Points

- All educational systems are built on standards, and teachers are accountable for the curriculum. As such, the curriculum is an excellent place to start when creating lessons for 21st-century fluency.

- To develop independent, lifelong learners, we must shift the burden of responsibility for learning from the teacher, where it has traditionally been, to the learner, where it truly belongs.

- Relevance must always be the top consideration in developing scenarios for learning to occur. If students can relate to it, if they can get excited about it, if they can connect to it, then they will learn from it.

- When scenarios are properly crafted, 21st-century fluencies will be cultivated as a natural part of the learning process.

Questions to Consider

- How do the 6 Ds (Define, Discover, Dream, Design, Deliver, and Debrief) relate to creating relevant lessons for students today?

- What real-world scenarios can you think of that could be used in your classroom?

- Why is it important to ensure that higher-level thinking is involved in our educational scenarios?

- What questions should you ask yourself when creating a scenario to ensure it is appropriate?

Chapter 12

The Committed Sardine

> Take the first step in faith. You don't have to see the whole staircase; just take the first step.
>
> Martin Luther King, Jr.

We must immediately begin to rethink and reshape the current classroom learning experience. This means we must re-examine the way we teach, the way students learn, and the way we assess that learning. We also acknowledge that this is a great challenge.

Think about it—how hard is it to break a small bad habit such as smoking, eating a bit too much chocolate, biting your nails, or being nominated to the Mastercard Hall of Fame? The answer is that it's really, really hard. But when we're challenged to rethink education, we're not being asked just to change a few bad habits like how we spend our money, what we put into our bodies, or how we spend our time. What we are being asked to do is reconsider some of the most fundamental, traditional, embedded parts of our life experience and our fundamental assumptions about how we teach, how students learn, and how that learning should be assessed.

The challenge we're facing in education at this time is that educators are being asked to reconsider our fundamental assumptions about how we teach, how students learn and how that learning should be assessed.

But when we're challenged to rethink education, we're not being asked just to change a few small behaviors or habits like how we spend our money, what we put into our bodies, or how we spend our time. What we are being asked to do here is reconsider some of the most fundamental, traditional, embedded parts of our life experiences and our habits of mind. And that is the real challenge that educators face.

And yes, change is hard. Sometimes the challenge of change seems absolutely overwhelming. So where do we begin? How do we in education deal with a world of such fast-paced change? How do we deal with embedded traditional mindsets about teaching and learning and assessment? How do we deal with the digital generation?

Facing the Music

It may seem a bit selfish, but what we passionately believe is that this is not about us; it's not about our issues; it's not about our comfort zone. This is about our children and our hopes and our dreams and our prayers for their future. They may only be 20 percent of the population, but they are 100 percent of the future of our nation.

Put on a more visceral level, all of our pension plans depend on how well we prepare them. Three billion new people entered the world economy in the past ten years, and if even if only ten percent of them have skills and opportunity to compete with us, that's still 300 million people—about twice the size of the entire U.S. workforce and twenty times the Canadian workforce.

In the work culture of the 21st century, everything from the neck down is going to be minimum wage. Everything that can be automated, turned into hardware, turned into

software, or outsourced or offshored will be. So we have a choice. Either our students and workers have high skills or they get low wages. And if they don't get those 21st-century skills in our schools, where will they get them?

We hear complaints all the time that kids today are different, and that our schools aren't what they used to be. Frankly, we believe the problem with our schools isn't that they aren't what they used to be. Culturally and socially they are different, but structurally, they are just like they were when students were released for 3 months in the summer so they could harvest the crops based on a European agricultural cycle from 150 years ago.

No, the problem is that our schools are what they used to be. So if we're going to prepare our students for their future and not just our past, if we're going to prepare them for their future and not just our comfort zone, we're going to need new schools—and more than that, we need a new mindset. We need new schools for the new world that awaits them. We need schools that will prepare students for their future—for life ahead of them after they leave school—for the rest of their lives. We know this is hard, but as educators, we must understand that our job is not just to serve what is or has been. Our job is to shape what can, what might, what absolutely must be.

Once again, change is difficult, and it's very easy to feel like you're overwhelmed by the magnitude of the changes required. But this is normal. Little has ever been understood or achieved in one blinding flash of light. The process of change is messy and doesn't happen overnight.

Honestly, in writing a book like *Literacy Is Not Enough*, and in creating a project as large as the 21st Century Fluency Project, it's easy to feel completely overwhelmed, and we certainly do feel that from time to time. But when we do feel overwhelmed, there's a place we like to go to decompress. That place is the Monterey Aquarium in Monterey, California. Some say it's the world's greatest aquarium.

The Joy of Whalewatching

A few years ago, Ian took his wife Nicky there for the first time. After they paid their fee, they walked inside. Immediately on their right was a gift shop that was playing a DVD about the blue whale, the largest and, at 190 decibels, the loudest mammal on earth, and is much louder than a person can shout (70 decibels) and louder than a jet (140 decibels). The video was full of amazing facts. The blue whale weighs more than a fully loaded 737. It is the length of 2 1/2 Greyhound buses put end to end and has a heart the size of a Volkswagen Beetle. It has blood vessels that a human adult could swim down and a tongue 8 feet long that weighs 6000 lbs. One particularly amazing fact was that in its first year of life, a baby blue whale was estimated to gain 15 pounds an hour.

One other amazing fact caught their attention—a blue whale is so mammoth that when it swims in one direction and it decides it needs to turn around, it takes three to five minutes to complete the turn.

There are a lot of people in our world who draw a strong parallel between the blue whale and the school system. And there are also a lot of people who believe that all the calls for charter schools and vouchers are being made by people who are wishing and hoping that we just won't be able to turn public education around in time.

But if you walk past the video on the blue whale, turn to the left and then walk about 50 yards down the way, you come to what we consider to be the absolute centerpiece of the Monterey Aquarium.

It's a 10 story, all-glass tank inside of which have been placed many of the creatures that are native to the Monterey Bay. If you've read ever John Steinbeck's *Cannery Row,* you'll know that a century ago, twice a year, in the inner Monterey Bay, there used to appear—out of nowhere—schools of sardines that were the length, the width, and the depth of city blocks. These immense crowds of the tiny fish had the mass not of one, two, or three blue whales, but of rather thousands of them.

But there is a fundamental difference between the way a blue whale turns around and a school of sardines changes its direction. How do they do it? How do they know? Is it ESP? Is it Twitter? Are they using cellphones?

Because we were quite curious, we pressed our noses against the tank and looked at the gigantic school of sardines swimming around inside.

At first glance, it looked like all the sardines were swimming in the same direction. But when our eyes adjusted to light, we began to realize, slowly at first, that at any one time there would be a small group of sardines swimming in another direction. And when they did this, they inevitably caused conflict, discomfort, collisions, and stress to each other.

But finally, when a critical mass of truly committed sardines was reached—not 50 or 60 percent who wanted to change, but 10 to 15 percent who truly believed in change, you know what happened? The rest of the school turned and followed. And that's exactly what has happened over the past few years with things like out attitudes toward smoking, our unwillingness to tolerate drinking and driving, or politicians who lie. It's exactly what happened with regime change in the Middle East. Each and every one of them was an overnight success that was years in the making. Every one of them started with a small group of people who were willing to make the change despite the obstacles and resistance.

You All Need To Be Committed!

On the 21st Century Fluency Project web site (www.fluency21.com) is our blog, which we call "The Committed Sardine Blog." When we first started posting we had a vision of building a following and providing world-class books and free resources that would help transform education to be relevant to life in the 21st century. We had a trickle of subscribers, which has turned into a flood. Today, we have tens of thousands of Committed Sardines in dozens of countries. The blog and resources have been accessed millions of times. Shortly it will expand into a personal learning network where you can create and share unit plans like the ones in this book.

So the big question is, who amongst you is willing to become a Committed Sardine? Who amongst you is willing to swim against the flow, against conventional wisdom, against our long-standing and traditional assumptions and practices in education and begin to move schools from where they are to where they need to be?

American anthropologist Maragret Mead put it this way:

"Never doubt that a small group of thoughtful committed people can change the world - indeed it is the only thing that ever has."

The bottom line is that change doesn't start with your president, change doesn't start with your governor, change doesn't start with your superintendent, and it doesn't start with your principal. Change starts with you and me, and we can't all change at once. And we can't just wait for everyone else to change first.

Change starts now. Change starts here. Change starts with me. Change starts with you. Remember that the longest journey starts with a single step. The greatest movement starts with a single individual. If it's going to be, it up to me, it's up to you, it's up to all of us.

Transforming schools is a great challenge. Sometimes the task does seem overwhelming and undoable. But stop for a moment to consider Helen Keller. She was someone who had great challenges in her life. She was a woman who was deaf, blind, and mute at the age of 15 months. But despite her profound—some would say unimaginable—disabilities, this woman earned her doctorate, became a college professor, wrote more than 30 books, and is widely considered to be one of the greatest thinkers of the past 100 years.

Later in her life, Helen Keller was approached by one of her students and asked a simple question: "Miss Keller, what is it like to be blind?" Helen Keller thought about this for a moment and responded as follows:

"The only thing worse than not being able to see, is being able to see and having no vision."

Isn't that exactly what *Literacy Is Not Enough* and the 21st-century fluencies are all about? It's not about looking back to what has been, but about looking forward to what learning and what the teaching and assessment of that learning can be. Try to keep this in mind as you think about the future and what we can do to prepare our children for the world that awaits them once they leave school.

The definition of insanity is doing the same thing you've always done but expecting, wanting, or needing something completely different. If we continue to do what we've always done, we'll continue to get the same results. We know the challenges you face today in your profession, both as educators and as people from an entirely different generation altogether. It is our responsibility—our *mission*—to ensure you don't face these challenges alone and unprepared.

You're the most important part of a young student's life. You're a worthy and experienced provider of knowledge, a giver of encouragement, and a nurturer of human potential. You are called upon in an age of uncertainty to be certain, and you are facing the greatest challenge we've ever faced, which is the challenge of change. Take pride in knowing that you can, and will, make a difference.

Solid Rock

a 21st Century Fluency Project

science grade **4**

10–12 periods

the big picture

Properties of Matter, Creative Teaching/Learning

the essential question

How can we use performing arts to teach the scientific properties of matter?

overview

Science unites with music in this fun and challenging lesson that engages students in learning about the properties of matter using song as their teaching method.

curricular objectives

- 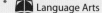 **McREL Science—Standard 12.—Level II—3.** Plans and conducts simple investigations (e.g., formulates a testable question, plans a fair test, makes systematic observations, develops logical conclusions).

- **McREL Thinking and Reasoning—Standard 4.—Level II—2.** Verifies the results of experiments.

- **McREL Science—Standard 8.— Level II—1.** Knows that matter has different states (i.e., solid, liquid, gas) and that each state has distinct physical properties; some common materials such as water can be changed from one state to another by heating or cooling.

- **McREL Science—Standard 8.— Level II—3.** Knows that substances can be classified by their physical and chemical properties (e.g., magnetism, conductivity, density, solubility, boiling and melting points).

- **McREL Science—Standard 8.— Level II—4.** Knows that materials may be composed of parts that are too small to be seen without magnification.

- **McREL Music—Standard 4.—Level II—2.**

- **McREL Language Arts—Standard 1.—Level II—1.**

- **McREL Language Arts—Standard 1.—Level II— 2.**

(For a full list of standards, see page 142.)

solution
fluency

information
fluency

creativity
fluency

media
fluency

collaboration
fluency

global digital
citizen

core concepts matrix

- properties of matter
- changing states of matter
- scientific inquiry/research
  - creative approaches to teaching

- À songwriting/music
- performing arts

* Language Arts   À Math   Science   Social Studies

Students will be writing and performing original songs based on teaching younger children about the scientific properties of matter.

High Tech: Students will write and produce a digital song using software such as GarageBand, accompanied by digital animations to illustrate key points.

Low Tech: Students will record an original song using standard recording equipment and collect photos and illustrations for a slideshow.

No Tech: Students will perform their song live and create graphics and illustrations using art materials.

the scenario

Matter is all around us in various different forms. Solids, liquids, and gases exist together in harmony to create the essence of our great planet. Ever wonder what this so-called matter is? Luckily for you, a local TV network that hosts a popular kids show has approached schools with a unique challenge. They want science classes in your grade level to work together to create a musical segment for their show.

The songs they are looking for must be entertaining but at the same time be an informative science lesson for kids about the properties of matter. The best song will be performed live and recorded for the show with a special audience of kids in attendance. So the question is, how would your class use research and inquiry to teach a subject like this to kids in a musical way that makes the knowledge stick in their minds?

Divide your class into three different musical groups—The Solids, The Liquids, and The Gases. The groups are working together to create this music segment for the kids show. Each group's challenge is to teach the kids about the specific states and physical properties they are representing using entertaining music and performance. Each group will do scientific research into the characteristics of its matter and how it relates to the other two. Then, each musical group will write a song that will be designed to teach kids about it on the new show being developed.

The songs should be anywhere from 2 to 3 minutes long and focus on a balance between instructional and entertainment value. Songs can be performed with or without instruments as accompaniment to an instructional slideshow, keynote, or animated cartoon. The songs can also be rendered digitally using a program such as GarageBand on the iPhone or iPad.

purposely withheld information

Students will be researching and discovering knowledge about the states and physical properties of matter for the purposes of teaching younger children about them. They will also be familiarizing themselves with the history of their discovery and the cultures/scientists credited for the research. They will be briefly researching how to write and record songs, if necessary, and using recording software if they choose to utilize it.

the learning process

exploring learner assumptions   1–2 periods

There are many different ways to present knowledge so that young minds remember it well for years afterward. Kids' programs use art, creativity, song, and storytelling to teach young children about life and the world around us. Ask the students to discuss how they would approach such a task. What would they need to consider in terms of the ages of their audience and their own artistic abilities? How would they decide on the best way to represent any kind of subject matter in a creative way that would resonate with young kids? Get them to discuss the importance of creativity, adventure, and relevance in learning as they think about how they would use creativity to teach younger children something valuable.

define   1–2 periods

Students work as a class to form musical groups that will write songs to teach kids about the state of matter and its properties, as part of a musical segment designed for a local kids TV show. Students have been presented with the lesson challenges and are required to provide a written definition of these challenges.

Prerequisites for Progression

Students have discussed the big picture and essential question as a group. In this lesson, students have learned that they will be doing the following:

- participate in one of three separate groups, writing an original song about the properties of one matter for an educational kids show

- research their chosen matter and learn about it and its properties

- write their songs in a way that teaches kids about the property they are representing

- perform it traditionally or in digital format as accompaniment to an instructional slideshow, keynote, or animation, or as a fully animated digital cartoon video

discover   1–2 periods

The class should form into three separate groups. The groups will familiarize themselves with the properties of matter by researching and collecting information for the purposes of teaching it to younger kids. In this lesson, they are playing the roles of songwriters, researchers, and instructors. They need to spend time discovering how they intend to approach each of these project tasks.

Prerequisites for Progression

Students have split into three separate groups and have conducted research on the subject matter. They have discussed how they will approach the creative, scientific, and instructional aspects of the project.

dream   1–2 periods

Each group is about to embark on a fun and creative personal journey into the world of science, tasked with being researchers, songwriters, and teachers. Each group will pool its research, scientific knowledge, and talents to write a song about the matter and its properties that the band name represents. This song will be part of a kids educational program. What kind of song would catch the attention of younger kids and help them learn about the subject matter? What kind of performance will help students remember the subject matter for a long time to come? Think about how you can make this lesson relevant, useful, and fun—both for yourselves and your young audience.

Prerequisites for Progression

Students have visualized how they will create an instructional song for kids on a specific state of matter and its properties. They have done research on their subject matter and collected information to develop their song content. They have discussed in their group how they will approach developing the task into a high-quality, creative, and instructional performance.

design   2–3 periods

It's time now for each group to begin placing their research into a song structure. It's important here to consider the target audience, which is younger kids. What kind of a song do you want to write to engage them in learning the scientific properties of matter that your song is about? What kind of visuals do you want to use? Will this be a completely digital performance rendered as an entertaining cartoon video? What about a live performance, perhaps using costumes and theatrics? It's up to your group to decide how you'll do it. But remember that your ultimate goal is an instructional one. That essentially means two things: first, you have to really know your subject matter; and second—and perhaps most important—you have to really think about a creative instructional approach that will make your lesson stick in a young person's mind and keep them interested.

Prerequisites for Progression

The student groups have begun to design and write their instructional songs and performances for the project. They are considering their audience and how best to create an effective project that teaches and entertains.

deliver—produce   2–3 periods

Each group will finalize their projects. This will require revision, rehearsal, and planning. They will need to revisit their projects to ensure that relevant and sufficient content is embedded in their song to get the message and teaching point across to younger children. Teaching creatively requires a good combination of vital information and artistic flair. The aim is to make both teaching and learning about the properties of matter fun while being educational.

Prerequisites for Progression

The groups have edited, revised, and finalized their song projects. They are ready to present them to the rest of the class or to an even larger audience.

the learning process

deliver—publish   2–3 periods

At this stage, each group will now present the performances of their songs in the format they've chosen. You can arrange for these performances to be presented in front of a larger audience than just the class. Your audience could comprise of much younger grades, which would be a good way of testing how these instructional songs teach their science lessons to younger kids. This might also be a good opportunity to put together an American Idol-style voting system for each performance. Students and larger audiences can vote on each performance using a Twitter feed or some other means of selection.

Prerequisites for Progression

The groups have performed their songs, and their performances have been assessed and/or voted on by a larger audience. They are ready to do a Debrief on the projects as a class.

debrief   1–2 periods

Have the class reflect on this fun lesson and share their experiences with each other. What have they discovered about creativity, and how is it vital to relevant learning? How much more memorable is the content when it is presented with artistic flair? Also, have students reflect on how they felt about being responsible for teaching this content to others. Did they find it easy or difficult? What were they required to do above and beyond simply researching scientific subjects for their songs? What did they have to consider to make the songs educational as well as entertaining? Would they have done anything differently? If so, what and why?

learning process formative rubric

define

above

_____

Students have discussed the big picture and essential question as a group. In this lesson, students have learned that they will be doing the following:

- **participate in one of three separate groups, writing an original song about the properties of one matter for an educational kids show**
- **research their chosen matter and learn about it and its properties**
- **write their songs in a way that teaches kids about the property they are representing**
- **perform it traditionally or in digital format as accompaniment to an instructional slideshow keynote or animation, or as a fully animated digital cartoon video**

below

_____

discover

above

_____

Students have split into three separate groups and have conducted research on the subject matter. They have discussed how they will approach the creative, scientific, and instructional aspects of the project.

below

_____

dream

above

_____

Students have visualized how they will create an instructional song for kids on a specific state of matter and its properties. They have done research on their subject matter and collected information to develop their song content. They have discussed in their group how they will approach developing the task into a high-quality, creative, and instructional performance.

below

_____

learning process formative rubric

design

above

The student groups have begun to design and write their instructional songs and performances for the project. They are considering their audience and how best to create an effective project that teaches and entertains.

below

---

deliver (produce)

above

The groups have edited, revised, and finalized their song projects. They are ready to present them to the rest of the class or to an even larger audience.

below

---

deliver (publish)

above

The groups have performed their songs, and their performances have been assessed and/or voted on by a larger audience. They are ready to do a Debrief on the project as a class.

below

4
The group members have created an original and unique song for their project that focuses on the property of matter that their group was representing. The content showed clear evidence of research into their subject matter. Their song was entertaining and educational, combining an instructional and creative approach that would appeal to younger kids in their song and performance. They made creative use of a visual component of images/animations/theatrics to illustrate their subject. They were able to answer all questions asked.

3
The group members have created a mostly original song for their project that focuses on the property of matter their group was representing. The content showed some evidence of research into their subject matter. Their song was mostly entertaining and educational, combining an instructional and creative approach that would appeal to younger kids in their song and performance. They made use of a visual component of images/animations/theatrics to illustrate their subject. They were able to answer most questions asked.

2
The group members have created a somewhat original song for their project that focuses partially on the property of matter their group was representing. The content showed limited evidence of research into their subject matter. Their song was somewhat entertaining and educational, somewhat combined an instructional and creative approach that would appeal to younger kids in their song and performance. They made some use of a visual component of images/animations/theatrics to illustrate their subject. They were able to answer some questions asked.

1
The group members have created a song with little originality for their project with little focus on the property of matter their group was representing. Their content showed little evidence of research on their subject matter. Their song was not entertaining or educational. They had little combination of an instructional and creative approach that would appeal to younger kids in their song and performance. They made little use of a visual component of images/animations/theatrics to illustrate their subject. They were able to answer few questions asked.

components rubric

4	3	2	1

song originality and focus

4	3	2	1
The group members have created an original and unique song that focuses on their property of matter.	The group members have created a mostly original song that focuses on their property of matter.	The group members have created a somewhat original song that focuses partially on their property of matter.	The group members have created a song with little originality or focus on their property of matter.

research

4	3	2	1
The content showed clear evidence of research into their subject matter.	The content showed some evidence of research into their subject matter.	The content showed limited evidence of research into their subject matter.	Their content showed little evidence of research into their subject matter.

approach—songwriting

4	3	2	1
Entertaining and educational, combining an instructional and creative approach.	Entertaining and educational, combining an instructional and creative approach.	Somewhat entertaining and educational, and combining an instructional and creative approach.	Little combination of an instructional and creative approach and was not entertaining or educational.

visual components

4	3	2	1
Creative use of a visual component of images/animations/theatrics to illustrate their subject.	Use of a visual component of images/animations/theatrics to illustrate their subject.	Some use of a visual component of images/animations/theatrics to illustrate their subject.	Little use of a visual component of images/animations/theatrics to illustrate their subject.

discussion

4	3	2	1
They were able to answer all questions asked.	They were able to answer most questions asked.	They were able to answer some questions asked.	They were able to answer few questions asked.

curricular objectives rubric—primary subject

above
_____
_____
_____

McREL Science—Standard 12.—Level II—3. Plans and conducts simple investigations (e.g., formulates a testable question, plans a fair test, makes systematic observations, develops logical conclusions).

below
_____
_____

above
_____
_____
_____

McREL Thinking/Reasoning—Standard 4.—Level II—2. Verifies the results of experiments.

below
_____
_____
_____

above
_____
_____
_____

McREL Science—Standard 8.— Level II—1. Knows that matter has different states (i.e., solid, liquid, gas) and that each state has distinct physical properties; some common materials such as water can be changed from one state to another by heating or cooling.

below
_____
_____
_____

above
_____
_____
_____

McREL Science—Standard 8.— Level II —3. Knows that substances can be classified by their physical and chemical properties (e.g., magnetism, conductivity, density, solubility, boiling and melting points).

below
_____
_____
_____

curricular objectives rubric—primary subject

above

below

McREL Science—Standard 8.— Level II —4. Knows that materials may be composed of parts that are too small to be seen without magnification.

above

McREL Music—Standard 4.—Level II—2. Creates and arranges short songs and instrumental pieces within specified guidelines (e.g., a particular style, form, instrumentation, compositional technique).

below

above

McREL Language Arts—Standard 1.—Level II—1. Prewriting: Uses prewriting strategies to plan written work (e.g., uses graphic organizers, story maps, and webs; groups related ideas; takes notes; brainstorms ideas; organizes information according to type and purpose of writing).

below

above

McREL Language Arts—Standard 1.—Level II— 2. Drafting and Revising: Uses strategies to draft and revise written work (e.g., elaborates on a central idea; writes with attention to audience, word choice, sentence variation; uses paragraphs to develop separate ideas; produces multiple drafts; selects punctuation for effect; eliminates redundancy).

below

above

McREL Language Arts—Standard 1.—Level II—6. Uses strategies (e.g., adapts focus, point of view, organization, form) to write for a variety of purposes (e.g., to inform, entertain, explain, describe, record ideas).

below

curricular objectives rubric—secondary subjects

above

McREL Music—Standard 6.—Level II—3. Identifies the sounds of a variety of instruments (e.g., orchestral, band, instruments from various cultures) and voices (e.g., male, female, children's voices).

below

above

McREL Music—Standard 1.—Level II—2. Sings expressively, with appropriate dynamics, phrasing, and interpretation.

below

above

McREL Music—Standard 2.—Level II—4. Performs in groups (e.g., blends instrumental timbres, matches dynamic levels, responds to the cues of a conductor).

below

above

McREL Music—Standard 3.—Level II—2. Improvises simple rhythmic variations and simple melodic embellishments on familiar melodies.

below

curricular objectives rubric—secondary subjects

above

McREL Behavioral Studies—Standard 1.—Level II—1. Understands that people can learn about others in many different ways (e.g., direct experience, mass communications media, conversations with others about their work and lives).

below

above

CC W.4.4. Produce clear and coherent writing in which the development and organization are appropriate to task, purpose, and audience.

below

above

CC W.4.5. With guidance and support from peers and adults, develop and strengthen writing as needed by planning, revising, and editing.

below

above

CC SL.4.5. Add audio recordings and visual displays to presentations when appropriate to enhance the development of main ideas or themes.

below

teacher/learner resources

Song: Properties of Matter
- http://gardenofpraise.com/matter.htm

Characteristic Properties of Matter
- http://www.stcms.si.edu/pom/pom_student_pt1.htm

Observable Properties of Matter
- http://www.chem1.com/acad/webtext/pre/matter.html

General Chemistry/Properties of Matter/Basic Properties of Matter
- http://en.wikibooks.org/wiki/General_Chemistry/Properties_of_Matter/Basic_Properties_of_Matter

The Particle Theory of Matter
- http://www.clickandlearn.org/gr9_sci/particle_theory.htm

Youtube: Properties of Matter—Science Experiments for Kids
- http://www.youtube.com/watch?v=pmHxYE_vDBs

Wikipedia: Matter
- http://en.wikipedia.org/wiki/Matter

Popular and Creative Teaching Ideas
- http://www.ehow.com/list_7232956_popular-creative-teaching-ideas.html

Arts-Based Approaches to Creative Teaching and Learning
- http://www.aare.edu.au/03pap/bur03114.pdf

Creative Teaching Ideas—The Art and Science of the Didactic Approach
- http://www.outdoor-nature-child.com/creative-teaching-ideas.html

Science Teaching Strategies
- http://www.starlasteachtips.com/sciencetips.html

iPods and Creativity in Learning and Teaching
- http://www.isetl.org/ijtlhe/pdf/IJTLHE20(1).pdf

Creative Teaching Tools
- http://www.helium.com/knowledge/159305-creative-teaching-tools

Creative Teaching and Learning: Historical, Political, and Institutional Perspectives
- http://opencreativity.open.ac.uk/assets/pdf/P%20WOODS%20AUG%2004.pdf

questions and ideas to expand this unit

cultivating global digital citizenship

- 🖥 ♟ Create educational songs and videos on other important subjects for different grade levels.

- 🖥 ♟ Produce and film a script for a scene or a short film that represents a significant aspect of student life at your school. Share it on a blog or web site, for viewing by other schools and students.

- 💔 ♟ Support local charities by organizing a school-wide talent show and collecting donations.

- 🖥 ♟ Create your own student-produced weekly kids program to help teach younger students about various curricular and non-curricular subjects.

 Personal Responsibility   Global Citizenship   Digital Citizenship   Altruistic Service   Environmental Stewardship

How can we make learning relevant and memorable, and why do you believe your ideas would work?

McREL Working With Others—Standard 4.—Level IV—3. Knows strategies to effectively communicate in a variety of settings (e.g., selects appropriate strategy for audience and situation).

McREL Working With Others—Standard 4.—Level IV—4. Provides feedback in a constructive manner, and recognizes the importance of seeking and receiving constructive feedback in a nondefensive manner.

Imagine a world without scientific knowledge. Define how we might explain the properties of matter in something other than scientific terms.

McREL Thinking and Reasoning—Standard 3.—Level II—1. Understands that one way to make sense of something is to think how it is like something more familiar.

McREL Visual Arts—Standard 3.—Level II—2. Knows how subject matter, symbols, and ideas are used to communicate meaning.

How can we apply art and storytelling to teach a variety of different subjects?

McREL Art Connections—Standard 1.—Level II—4. Knows ways in which the principles and subject matter of other disciplines taught in the school are interrelated with those of the arts (e.g., pattern in the arts and in science).

McREL Visual Arts—Standard 3.—Level II—2. Knows how subject matter, symbols, and ideas are used to communicate meaning.

McREL Thinking and Reasoning—Standard 3.—Level II—1. Understands that one way to make sense of something is to think how it is like something more familiar.

questions and ideas to expand this unit

How can things like science and art help us learn about other cultures?

McREL Behavioral Studies—Standard 1.—Level II—1. Understands that people can learn about others in many different ways (e.g., direct experience, mass communications media, conversations with others about their work and lives).

McREL Behavioral Studies—Standard 3.—Level II—5. Knows that learning means using what one already knows to make sense out of new experiences or information, not just storing the new information in one's head.

notes and thoughts

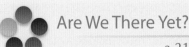 Are We There Yet?

a 21st Century Fluency Project

 math △ grade **6**

10–12 periods

the big picture

Fuel Economy/Energy Conservation

the essential question

How can you analyze vehicle fuel economy to find a great car that both protects the environment and saves you money?

overview

Students work individually to create a poster that displays information about the "car of their dreams." In addition to pictures and basic information about the car, the poster includes a graph, table, and road trip plan relating fuel efficiency statistics to other factors such as distance traveled and fuel costs.

curricular objectives

△ **CC 6.RP.2.** Understand the concept of a unit rate a/b associated with a ratio a:b with b ≠ 0, and use rate language in the context of a ratio relationship.

△ **CC 6.RP.3.** Use ratio and rate reasoning to solve real-world and mathematical problems.

△ **CC 6.RP.3.a.** Make tables of equivalent ratios relating quantities with whole-number measurements, find missing values in the tables, and plot the pairs of values on the coordinate plane. Use tables to compare ratios.

△ **CC 6.RP.3.b.** Solve unit rate problems including those involving unit pricing and constant speed.

△ **CC 6.NS.3.** Fluently add, subtract, multiply, and divide multi-digit decimals using the standard algorithm for each operation.

📖 **CC RL.6.1.** Cite textual evidence to support analysis of what the text says explicitly as well as inferences drawn from the text.

📖 **CC W.6.2.** Write informative/explanatory texts to examine a topic and convey ideas, concepts, and information through the selection, organization, and analysis of relevant content.

📖 **CC RH.6-8.7.** Integrate visual information (e.g., in charts, graphs, photographs, videos, or maps) with other information in print and digital texts.

(For a full list of standards, see page 161.)

solution fluency

information fluency

 creativity fluency

media fluency

 collaboration fluency

core concepts matrix

△ understand ratios and unit rates

🔬 △ use ratios to compare costs

📖 △ areas of triangles/quadrilaterals

△ use unit rates to solve problems

△ plot pairs of values from the tables on the coordinate plane

 global digital citizen

* 📖 Language Arts △ Math 🔬 Science 🌐 Social Studies

Students create a poster about a car they would like to own. The poster must include a graph that displays miles-per-gallon information, a table that shows cost for fuel the vehicle will use, and a detailed plan for a road trip that includes information about fuel expenses.

High Tech: Students use block-poster software to transfer high-resolution graphics and pictures to a wall-sized image.

Low Tech: Students use graphics and photo-editing software to produce a large poster.

No Tech: Students draw graphs and cut and paste images from the Internet on poster board.

the scenario

Although it is still a few years until you are eligible to get a driver's license, you may already be thinking about what type of car you'd like to drive. Gas-powered? Hybrid? Electric? There is even a new car that flies!

It's predicted that gasoline prices will continue to rise, so fuel economy will be an even greater factor to consider in the future when buying a car. You decide to start researching vehicle fuel economy now so that you can start saving up money to purchase a great car that is fuel efficient.

Your challenge is to make a poster titled "Car of My Dreams" that will motivate you to start saving for a car. The poster, which you plan to hang on your bedroom wall, will show pictures of the car you want to buy. In addition to pictures of the car, your poster will include the following: (a) a graph on the coordinate plane that uses ratios to relate fuel used and miles traveled, (b) a table giving information about projected cost based on unit rate for the type of fuel your car will use, and (c) a detailed plan for a road trip that includes calculations for what fuel costs will be. Upon completion, you will present your poster to teacher(s) and classmates at an "unveiling" event.

So rev up your engines and get started on your poster now. Begin by visiting the U.S. Department of Energy's web site at www.fueleconomy.gov, where you'll find all kinds of data, including miles per gallon (MPG) information about present-day cars as well as cars of the future.

purposely withheld information

Students research how statistics on fuel economy are calculated and gain an understanding of how the given statistics relate to the information they need for their poster. They will need to determine what sources they will use for fuel economy information and assess how reliable those sources are. Students will need to investigate how to use Photoshop or other image-editing software to create wall-sized posters from images that fit on their computer screens. Students will decide on specifics such as size and layout of their posters, as well as the format of their presentations at the unveiling event.

the learning process

exploring learner assumptions   1–2 periods

Students are likely to have preconceptions about fuel economy from media reports about government regulations, advertisements for new vehicles, and information gleaned from parents and other family members who are shopping for cars. Have them discuss and share these preconceptions. Make them aware that, for this project, they will need to be meticulous in their understanding of what fuel economy statistics really mean. Some students may have already decided on the type or make of car they want, even if that car is currently not very fuel efficient. Have them talk about why they have decided on that particular car. By investigating proposed improvements for vehicle fuel efficiency in the near future, students may find that fuel economy will be greatly improved by the time they are ready to buy a car.

define   1–2 periods

Students will produce a wall-sized poster using high-resolution graphics and images created on their computers. The poster must be unique and motivating, showing all the information in a clear and comprehensible format. In addition to showing pictures of the car the student wants to buy, the poster will include a graph on the coordinate plane, a table about projected cost, and a detailed plan for a road trip. After the class discussion, present students with the scenario and essential question. Ask students to individually produce a written definition of the challenges.

Prerequisites for Progression

Students fully understand the expectations for creating the poster and the details they need to have. They have created a written definition of the challenge. They know they will be creating an original poster idea detailing a car they would like to own. The poster must include a graph that displays miles-per-gallon information on the coordinate plane, a table that shows projected unit cost for fuel the vehicle will use, and a detailed plan for a road trip that includes information about fuel expenses. They may render their project using digital design software, photo-editing, or standard art materials.

discover   2–3 periods

Students begin to explore different types of cars and how the cars rate in regard to fuel economy. They learn about innovative technology, from mainstream advances such as hybrid and electric cars to more unconventional approaches such as hydrogen-powered autos and vegetable-fueled "greasecars." Students will need to delve into the meaning behind fuel economy statistics to understand the effects of the different factors on the numbers, such as whether the car is being driven on the highway or in a city. Students also begin to familiarize themselves with imaging software to help them create a wall-sized poster from a file on their computer.

Prerequisites for Progression

Students have done background research on different types of cars and measurements of fuel economy and have started familiarizing themselves with imaging software for creating their posters.

the learning process

dream   1–2 periods

After exploring fuel economy for different types of cars, students envision themselves at the wheel of the car of their dreams. For some students, this car may be sold at a cost far above any amount they could save. For other students, this car may be a vehicle they would like to build themselves if they could acquire the technological know-how. Given the high price of most cars these days, students may become discouraged when they start to learn about the costs of owning and running a car. Ask students if they think that improved fuel economy could make a vehicle with a higher price tag actually less expensive to own in the long run. As students begin to think about planning their road trip, encourage them to think about how they can use ratios for fuel used and miles traveled to develop a budget for the fuel costs of their trip.

Prerequisites for Progression

Students have started identifying the car they will feature on their poster and are analyzing the relationship between fuel economy and the long-term cost of the car.

design   2–3 periods

Students decide on the car to feature in their poster and develop a timeline for production. They gather the relevant fuel economy statistics, design their table and graph, and plan their road trip. They sketch out the layout for their poster to allow them to transfer the design on their computer screen to a much larger image. Students plan what they will do and say in the presentation.

Prerequisites for Progression

Students have identified the car for their poster and have developed a realistic timeline for producing the poster.

deliver—produce   2–3 periods

The poster is completed. Encourage students to revisit each stage of the process, examining how they incorporated fuel economy statistics into their display and how they used ratios and unit rates in their tables, graphs, and road trip plans. Advise students to ask classmates for feedback before presenting the final version of their poster.

Prerequisites for Progression

Students have collected and analyzed all fuel economy statistics for their car, incorporated this information in their poster, and taken into account feedback.

the learning process

deliver—publish   2–3 periods

Students present their posters to teacher(s) and classmates, who provide feedback addressing the effectiveness of the poster in displaying information about the car. Assessment of mathematical content focuses on how clearly and accurately ratios and unit rates are used to show the relationship between fuel economy and quantities such as miles traveled and fuel costs. The following are criteria that may be used in assessment. Has the student:

- Collected accurate and relevant information about the fuel economy for his or her car?
- Included a graph on the coordinate plane that uses ratios to relate fuel used and miles traveled?
- Created a table giving information about projected cost based on unit rate for the type of fuel the car will use?
- Shown a detailed plan for a road trip that includes calculations for what fuel costs will be?
- Displayed all required information on a poster, using appropriate images and graphics?
- Presented his or her poster to the class and listened to feedback from instructor(s) and peers?

Questions that may be asked by teachers for purposes of assessment include:

- How did you decide which car would be the "car of your dreams"?
- What do you think about the fuel efficiency of your car?
- What are some of the factors that can affect fuel efficiency?
- How did you make design decisions about the layout and content of your poster?

Prerequisites for Progression

Students have presented their posters and had them critiqued by instructor(s) and peers based on their design, the accuracy of data collected, and the correct usage of ratios and unit rates.

debrief   1–2 periods

Students reflect on the critiques they have received from instructor(s) and peers and make revisions based on suggestions they receive. Students will discuss the project as a group, reflecting on the strategies they used for gathering information about fuel economy and analyzing the specific statistics for their cars. Ask students to review their use of ratios and unit rates as they created their graphs, tables, and road trip plans. How did the miles-per-gallon ratio help them create the graph in the coordinate plane? How did unit rates help them calculate costs for their road trip? What aspects of designing and producing the poster went smoothly? What, if anything, would they have done differently?

learning process formative rubric

define

above

Students fully understand the expectations for creating the poster and the details they need to have. They have created a written definition of the challenge.

below

discover

above

Students have done background research on different types of cars and measurements of fuel economy and have started familiarizing themselves with imaging software for creating their posters.

below

dream

above

Students have started identifying the car they will feature on their poster and are analyzing the relationship between fuel economy and the long-term cost of the car.

below

design

above

Students have identified the car for their poster and have developed a realistic timeline for producing the poster.

below

learning process formative rubric

deliver (produce)

above

_____
_____
_____

Students have collected and analyzed all fuel economy statistics for their car, incorporated this information in their poster, and taken into account feedback.

below

_____
_____
_____

deliver (publish)

above

_____
_____
_____

Students have collected and analyzed all fuel economy statistics for their car, incorporated this information in their poster, and taken into account feedback.

below

_____
_____
_____

4

The individual student has created a unique and motivating poster that displays all information about the chosen car, including fuel economy statistics and other data, in a clear and comprehensible format. The poster includes all of the following: (a) a graph on the coordinate plane that uses ratios to relate fuel used and miles traveled, (b) a table giving information about projected cost based on unit rate for the type of fuel the car will use, and (c) a detailed plan for a road trip that includes calculations for what fuel costs will be. All information and calculations are shown with 100% accuracy. The design and layout of the poster makes it easy to understand and interpret the given information. The student is able to answer all of the questions asked at the time of delivery.

3

The individual student has created a motivating poster that displays all information about the chosen car, including fuel economy statistics and other data, in a comprehensible format. The poster includes all of the following: (a) a graph on the coordinate plane that uses ratios to relate fuel used and miles traveled, (b) a table giving information about projected cost based on unit rate for the type of fuel the car will use, and (c) a detailed plan for a road trip that includes calculations for what fuel costs will be. All information and calculations are shown with at least 80% accuracy. The design and layout of the poster makes it easy to understand the given information. The student was able to answer most of the questions asked at the time of delivery.

2

The individual student has created a poster that displays all information about the chosen car, including fuel economy statistics and other data, in a comprehensible format. The poster includes all of the following: (a) a graph on the coordinate plane that uses ratios to relate fuel used and miles traveled, (b) a table giving information about projected cost based on unit rate for the type of fuel the car will use, and (c) a detailed plan for a road trip that includes calculations for what fuel costs will be. All information and calculations are shown with at least 60% accuracy. The design and layout of the poster makes it possible to understand the given information. The student was able to answer some of the questions asked at the time of delivery.

1

The individual student has created a poster that displays information about the chosen car, including fuel economy statistics and other data. The poster includes all of the following: (a) a graph on the coordinate plane that uses ratios to relate fuel used and miles traveled, (b) a table giving information about projected cost based on unit rate for the type of fuel the car will use, and (c) a detailed plan for a road trip that includes calculations for what fuel costs will be. All information and calculations are shown with less than 60% accuracy. The design and layout of the poster makes it difficult to understand the given information. The student was able to answer few of the questions asked at the time of delivery.

components rubric

4   3   2   1

poster format

4	3	2	1
The individual student has created a unique and motivating poster with a clear and comprehensible format.	The individual student has created a motivating poster with a comprehensible format.	The individual student has created a poster with a comprehensible format.	The individual student has created a poster.

car information

4	3	2	1
All information collected about the car is 100% accurate.	Information collected about the car may contain minor errors but is at least 80% accurate.	Information collected about the car contains errors but is at least 60% accurate.	Information collected about the car contains errors and is less than 60% accurate.

ratio and unit accuracy

4	3	2	1
All ratios and unit rates have been used with 100% accuracy.	The use of ratios and unit rates may include some minor errors but is at least 80% accurate.	The use of ratios and unit rates includes errors but is at least 60% accurate.	The use of ratios and unit rates includes errors and is less than 60% accurate.

graph and table accuracy

4	3	2	1
The relationship between fuel used and miles traveled and projected fuel cost is shown with 100% accuracy.	The relationship between fuel used and miles traveled and projected fuel cost is shown with at least 80% accuracy.	The relationship between fuel used and miles traveled and projected fuel cost is shown with at least 60% accuracy.	The relationship between fuel used and miles traveled and projected fuel cost is shown with less than 60% accuracy.

The relationship between fuel used and miles traveled and projected fuel cost is shown with less than 60% .

4	3	2	1
Calculations of fuel costs for the road trip are 100% accurate.	Calculations of fuel costs for the road trip contain minor errors but are at least 80% accurate.	Calculations of fuel costs for the road trip contain errors but are at least 60% accurate.	Calculations of fuel costs for the road trip contain errors and are less than 60% accurate.

components rubric

4	3	2	1

layout design

4	3	2	1
The design and layout of the poster makes it easy to understand and interpret the given information.	The design and layout of the poster makes it easy to understand the given information.	The design and layout of the poster makes it possible to understand the given information.	The design and layout of the poster makes it difficult to understand the given information.

discussion

4	3	2	1
The student is able to answer all of the questions asked at the time of delivery.	The student was able to answer most of the questions asked at the time of delivery.	The student was able to answer most of the questions asked at the time of delivery.	The student was able to answer few of the questions asked at the time of delivery.

curricular objectives rubric—primary subject

above

CC 6.RP.2. Understand the concept of a unit rate a/b associated with a ratio a:b with b ≠ 0, and use rate language in the context of a ratio relationship.

below

above

CC 6.RP.3. Use ratio and rate reasoning to solve real-world and mathematical problems.

below

above

CC 6.RP.3.a. Make tables of equivalent ratios relating quantities with whole-number measurements, find missing values in the tables, and plot the pairs of values on the coordinate plane. Use tables to compare ratios.

below

above

CC 6.RP.3.b. Solve unit rate problems including those involving unit pricing and constant speed.

below

above

_____

_____

_____

CC 6.NS.3. Fluently add, subtract, multiply, and divide multi-digit decimals using the standard algorithm for each operation.

below

_____

_____

_____

curricular objectives rubric—secondary subjects

above

CC RH.6-8.7. Integrate visual information (e.g., in charts, graphs, photographs, videos, or maps) with other information in print and digital texts.

below

above

CC RL.6.1. Cite textual evidence to support analysis of what the text says explicitly as well as inferences drawn from the text.

below

above

CC W.6.2. Write informative/explanatory texts to examine a topic and convey ideas, concepts, and information through the selection, organization, and analysis of relevant content.

below

above

CC W.6.2.a. Introduce a topic; organize ideas, concepts, and information, using strategies such as definition, classification, comparison/contrast, and cause/effect; include formatting (e.g., headings), graphics (e.g., charts, tables), and multimedia when useful to aiding comprehension.

below

curricular objectives rubric—secondary subjects

above

CC W.6.2.b. Develop the topic with relevant facts, definitions, concrete details, quotations, or other information and examples; c. Use appropriate transitions to clarify the relationships among ideas and concepts.

below

above

CC W.6.7. Conduct short research projects to answer a question (including a self-generated question), drawing on several sources and generating additional related, focused questions that allow for multiple avenues of exploration.

below

teacher/learner resources

U.S. Department of Energy—www.fueleconomy.gov

Corporate Average Fuel Economy Overview—http://www.nhtsa.gov/cars/rules/cafe/overview.htm

U.S. Environmental Protection Agency Fuel Economy Site—http://www.epa.gov/fueleconomy/index.htm

Greasecar Vegetable Fuel Systems—http://www.greasecar.com

MIT Engineers' Flying Car—http://web.mit.edu/newsoffice/2009/flying-car-0319.html

Fossil Fuels—http://fossil.energy.gov/index.html

Fuels of the Future—http://www.futurecars.com/future_fuels.html

Two-Lane Highway Road Trips—http://www.roadtripusa.com/

Energy Conservation Tips for Cars—http://www.livestrong.com/article/155836-energy-conservation-tips-for-cars/

Tribal Energy and Environmental Information Clearinghouse—http://teeic.anl.gov/er/conserve/conservevehicle/index.cfm

My Car Stats—http://www.mycarstats.com/content/car_fuel_economy_why.asp

How Can I Improve My Gas Mileage?—http://www.improve-gas-mileage-guide.com/

Hybrids—http://www.hybridcars.com/

Gas vs. Diesel vs. Hybrid Power

- http://what-when-how.com/energy-engineering/greenhouse-gas-emissions-gasoline-hybrid-electric-and-hydrogen-fueled-vehicles-energy-engineering/
- http://editorial.autos.msn.com/article.aspx?cp-documentid=435228
- http://www.biodieselathome.net/Gasoline_Prices/Gasoline_Prices_And_Hybrid_Cars.html
- http://www.physorg.com/news10031.html
- http://www.favstocks.com/electric-cars-hybrid-cars-or-high-mpg-gas-powered-cars/0854956/
- http://www.financialnewsline.com/leasing/the-hybrid-car-and-gas-prices/
- http://www.carseek.com/articles/hybrid-vs-gas.html

Fuel Efficiency

- http://banktime.com/auto/the-truth-about-fuel-economy/1283/
- http://www.secureonlineorder.net/tpepublic/term-papers/15685_Car_Fuel_Efficiency.pdf

Gasoline and Diesel Fuel Update—http://www.eia.doe.gov/oog/info/gdu/gasdiesel.asp

Road Trip Calculator

- http://www.roadtripamerica.com/fuel-cost-calculator.php
- http://www.tripcalculator.org/

resources

teacher/learner resources

Global Geopolitics—http://globalgeopolitics.net/

Automobile Fuel Economy Standards—http://www.rff.org/documents/RFF-DP-10-45.pdf

Factors Contributing to Fuel Economy

- http://www.driverside.com/auto-library/top_10_factors_contributing_to_fuel_economy-317
- http://www.omninerd.com/articles/Improve_MPG_The_Factors_Affecting_Fuel_Efficiency

Fuel Economy on Environmental Issues

- http://environment.about.com/od/fossilfuels/a/fuel_label.htm
- http://www.nutramed.com/environment/cars.htm

questions and ideas to expand this unit

cultivating global digital citizenship

🌱 💻 ❗ Explore vehicle fuels of the future and identify the impact of these new fuels on issues such as car design and infrastructure for fueling stations.

🌱 💻 ❗ Keep track of fuel used, miles traveled, and fuel costs for your family vehicle for a month. Issue a report on your findings.

🌱 💻 ❗ Quantify vehicle fuel usage as a percentage of overall energy use, contribution to carbon emissions, and other environmental measures. Investigate other factors that contribute to these measures.

*   Personal Responsibility   Global Citizenship   Digital Citizenship   Altruistic Service   Environmental Stewardship

How could you use the type of information you displayed on your poster to create a web site comparing fuel economy for different makes and models of cars?

CC RH.6-8.7. Integrate visual information (e.g., in charts, graphs, photographs, videos, or maps) with other information in print and digital texts.

How could you use the information you gathered about fuel economy of cars to further your understanding of more general environmental issues?

McREL Science—Standard 12.—Level III—7. Establishes relationships based on evidence and logical argument (e.g., provides causes for effects).

What impact does vehicle fuel economy have on global geopolitics?

McREL Geography—Standard 6.—Level III—2. Knows how technology affects the ways in which culture groups perceive and use places and regions (e.g., impact of technology such as air conditioning and irrigation on the human use of arid lands; changes in perception of environment by culture groups, such as the snowmobile's impact on the lives of Inuit people or the swamp buggy's impact on tourist travel in the Everglades)

How do increases and decreases in vehicle fuel costs affect prices of other consumer products?

McREL Economics—Standard 3.—Level III—2. Understands that relative prices and how they affect people's decisions are the means by which a market system provides answers to the basic economic questions: What goods and services will be produced? How will they be produced? Who will buy them?

notes and thoughts

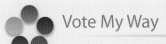

Vote My Way
a 21st Century Fluency Project

social studies | grade **8**

12–15 periods

the big picture

Role of Powerful Associations in Politics, Bias in Propaganda

the essential question

What would be the important contributing factors that would give a running candidate the best chance of winning an election?

overview

Students will research how an organization has supported candidates and used their position to try to influence voters over the past 20 years through an interview with that organization and through examining their pieces of propaganda. They will then choose a potential candidate for the organization to support in the next election and create a persuasive TV ad and podcast.

curricular objectives

- 🌐 **McRel Civics—Standards 20.—Level III—4.** Understands the historical and contemporary roles of prominent associations and groups in local, state, and national politics (e.g., historical associations such as abolitionists, suffragists, labor unions, civil rights groups; religious organizations and contemporary associations such as AFL-CIO, National Education Association, Common Cause, League of Women Voters, Greenpeace, National Association for the Advancement of Colored People).

- 🌐 **McREL Civics—Standard 13.—Level III—4.** Knows reasons why most political conflict in the United States has generally been less divisive than in many other nations (e.g., a shared respect for the Constitution and its principles, a sense of unity within diversity, willingness to relinquish power when voted out of office, willingness to use the legal system to manage conflicts, opportunities to improve one's economic condition).

- 🌐 **McREL Geography—Standard 4.—Level III—1.** Knows the human characteristics of places (e.g., cultural characteristics such as religion, language, politics, technology, family structure, gender; population characteristics; land uses; levels of development).

- 🌐 **McREL Behavioral Studies—Standard 1.—Level III—2.**

- ⌨ **McREL Technology—Standard 3.—Level III—8.**

(For a full list of standards, see page 178.)

solution fluency

information fluency

creativity fluency

media fluency

collaboration fluency

global digital citizen

core concepts matrix

- 📖 🌐 bias in media
- 📖 🌐 persuasive language
- 📖 persuasive writing/speech
- 📖 Å graphic design/layout

- 📖 🌐 campaign strategies
- 📖 🌐 political organizations and groups

---

*  Language Arts   Math   Science   Social Studies

setting the scene

Students will explore how an organization has affected political campaigns over the past 20 years, specifically exploring the tactics, wording, and techniques they have used in propaganda.

High Tech: Students will conduct a Skype interview with a member of the organization. They will write, produce, and record the persuasive TV ad and digitally record a podcast to be revealed at their press conference.

Low Tech: Students will conduct an email interview with a member of the organization. They will write, produce, and videotape the persuasive TV ad and tape record a podcast to be revealed at their press conference.

No Tech: Students will conduct an in-person or phone interview with a member of the organization. They will write, produce, and perform the persuasive TV ad and perform a live podcast to be revealed at their press conference.

the scenario

The presidential election is just around the corner and the ads on TV are becoming overwhelming. Every day there is a new ad with information that conflicts with what was said yesterday. Different organizations are airing new and negative ads about each candidate continuously. It seems as though the one thing everyone can agree on is that it is getting impossible to know whom to believe.

Your challenge is to explore the roles bias has played in campaigning; specifically, how prominent groups can sway popular opinion. Your group will choose an organization that has a strong political voice and examine how they have supported different candidates for the past 20 years. Explore all aspects of their propaganda—television ads, radio ads, print materials, social media, and so on—to see what correlations you can find in the tactics, wording, and techniques they have used to convince voters. Arrange a Skype, email, phone, or in-person interview with a member of the organization. What are the issues that matter to your organization? How did they select which candidate to support? In what ways has the organization promoted or supported the candidates they believe in? Have their methods stayed the same over time or have they evolved? During a campaign, have they changed approaches, and if so, has that been affective? Has the role of the organization gained or lessened depending on the current political climate?

Using a current list of people announced to be or considering running for the office of the president, select the next candidate that you believe the organization will support and create your first round of propaganda for that candidate, including a persuasive television ad and podcast. Make sure to create these in the style used by the organization in past pieces. You will then host a press conference announcing the candidate and unveiling the campaign materials.

purposely withheld information

Students might not be aware of what political ads are not created/paid for by the candidate, but by different organizations supporting them. Students may also be not be aware that organizations will support different parties, often simultaneously, due to a specific issue. Students may also assume that an organization may only voice their support for a candidate and not realize that the organization may actively campaign against an opposing candidate.

the learning process

exploring learner assumptions   1–2 periods

Have a discussion with the students about what organizations they think have had strong opinions on political campaigns. Why do they believe an organization would want to support a specific candidate as opposed to a specific issue? What factors do they think the organization would use to decide which candidate to back? What kinds of methods to they think the organizations has used to voice their support?

define   1–2 periods

The scenario has been presented to the students. Students are asked to explore how an organization has supported candidates and used their position to try and influence voters over the past 20 years, and then choose a potential candidate for the organization to support in the next election, and create a persuasive TV ad and podcast. They will also host a press conference, where they will unveil their campaign materials. Groups have been assigned, and the students have selected the organization they will focus on. To ensure students understand the challenges they face in this unit, ask them to submit a written definition.

Prerequisites for Progression

The students have created a written definition of the problem that includes the following: Explore how an organization has supported candidates and used their position to try and influence voters over the past 20 years. Next, conduct an interview with a member of that organization, and examine the various forms of propaganda, paying specific attention to the tactics, wording, and techniques utilized in them, as well as the outcomes of those campaigns. Utilizing this information and criteria, choose a potential candidate for the organization to support in the next election, and create a persuasive TV ad and podcast. Students will also host a press conference, where students will unveil their campaign materials.

discover   2–3 periods

In this stage, students research their organization's support of political candidates and influence on voters over the past 20 years. The students look at all aspects of their propaganda—television ads, radio ads, print materials, social media, and so on—to see what correlations they can find in the tactics, wording, and techniques they have used to convince voters. The students arrange and conduct a Skype, email, phone, or in-person interview with a member of the organization. Questions include: What are the issues that matter to your organization? How did the organization select which candidate to support? In what ways has the organization promoted or supported the candidates they believe in? Have their methods stayed the same over time, or have they evolved? During a campaign, have they changed approaches, and if so, has that been affective? Has the role of the organization gained or lessened depending on the current political climate? Students will also identify current presidential candidates (or people considering/ rumored to be running in the next election).

Prerequisites for Progression

The students researched their organization's support of political candidates and influence on voters over the past 20 years. The students looked at their propaganda to find correlations in the tactics, wording, and techniques used to convince voters and conducted an interview with a member of the organization. The students identified potential presidential candidates for the next election.

dream   1–2 periods

Students will now begin to consider the candidate they believe their organization would choose to support. What are the ideals or qualities this candidate has that make them a match for the organization? How does this person compare to successful candidates the organization has supported in the past? Around this candidate, they will begin to build a first round of campaign propaganda for their persuasive television ad and a podcast in the style of their organization. They will pay particular attention to the tactics, wording, and techniques used in the past by the organization. Are there specific tactics or techniques that seem to work better? What effect did current events have on the tactics or language selected?

Prerequisites for Progression

Students have selected their candidate and identified the style and qualities of the propaganda they will create for that candidate.

design   2–3 periods

Students will write the scripts for the persuasive television ad and podcast. They will design and create any production elements they need according to the demands of their formats and rehearse the performances of the television ad and the podcast.

Prerequisites for Progression

The students have written, selected, and prepared all of the elements of their persuasive television ad and podcast.

deliver—produce   2–3 periods

The students will now rehearse and, if required, record their persuasive television ad and podcast.

Prerequisites for Progression

Students have prepared their persuasive television ads and podcast for presentation at their press conference according to their selected formats.

deliver—produce   2–3 periods

Students will now share the persuasive television ad and podcast during their press conference.

Prerequisites for Progression

The students have hosted their press conference and presented their persuasive television ad and podcast.

the learning process

debrief 1–2 periods

Have a discussion as to what the students' reaction was to different campaigns. Did they feel their opinions on a particular candidate were affected by either the information presented or the style in which the candidate was presented? What would they identify as the main stylistic traits of each organization? What kinds of word choices or tactics did they find different organizations using similarly? Were there differences in how different organizations presented the information that surprised them? Were there differing tactics that organizations used to make the same point? Did they react more strongly to positive or negative tactics or words?

learning process formative rubric

define

above
_____
_____
_____

The students have created a written definition of the problem that includes the following: Explore how an organization has supported candidates and used their position to try and influence voters over the past 20 years. Next, conduct an interview with a member of that organization, and examine the various forms of propaganda, paying specific attention to the tactics, wording, and techniques utilized in them as well as the outcomes of those campaigns. Utilizing this information and criteria, choose a potential candidate for the organization to support in the next election and create a persuasive TV ad and podcast. Students will also host a press conference, where they will unveil their campaign materials.

below
_____
_____
_____

discover

above
_____
_____
_____

The students researched their organization's support of political candidates and influence on voters over the past 20 years. The students looked at their propaganda to find correlations in the tactics, wording, and techniques used to convince voters and conducted an interview with a member of the organization. The students identified potential presidential candidates for the next election.

below
_____
_____
_____

dream

above
_____
_____
_____

Students have selected their candidate and identified the style and qualities of the propaganda they will create for that candidate.

below
_____
_____
_____

learning process formative rubric

design

above

_____

The students have written, selected, and prepared all of the elements of their persuasive television ad and podcast.

below

_____

deliver (produce)

above

_____

Students have prepared their persuasive television ads and podcast for presentation at their press conference according to their selected formats.

below

_____

deliver (publish)

above

_____

The students have hosted their press conference and presented their persuasive television ad and podcast.

below

_____

4

The students thoroughly explored how an organization has supported candidates and used their position to try and influence voters over the past 20 years. They conducted a detailed interview with multiple members of that organization and examined all or a majority of the organization's propaganda, paying specific attention to the tactics, wording, and techniques utilized in them as well as the outcomes of those campaigns. Utilizing this information and criteria, the students chose a well-matched potential candidate for the organization to support in the next election. The students created a unique, compelling, and persuasive television ad and podcast, which they unveiled at their press conference.

3

The students explored how an organization has supported candidates and used their position to try and influence voters over the past 20 years. They conducted a detailed interview with a member of that organization and examined most of the organization's propaganda, paying specific attention to the tactics, wording, and techniques utilized in them as well as the outcomes of those campaigns. Utilizing this information and criteria, the students chose a suitable potential candidate for the organization to support in the next election. The students created a compelling and persuasive television ad and podcast, which they unveiled at their press conference.

2

The students partially explored how an organization has supported candidates and used their position to try and influence voters over the past 20 years. They conducted a basic interview with a member of that organization and examined some of the organization's propaganda, paying specific attention to the tactics, wording, and techniques utilized in them as well as the outcomes of those campaigns. Utilizing this information and criteria, the students chose a partially suitable potential candidate for the organization to support in the next election. The students created a somewhat persuasive television ad and podcast, which they unveiled at their press conference.

1

The students did not explore how an organization has supported candidates and used their position to try and influence voters over the past 20 years. They conducted a non-detailed interview with a member of that organization and examined a few of the organization's propaganda, paying little attention to the tactics, wording, and techniques utilized in them as well as the outcomes of those campaigns. Utilizing this information and criteria, the students chose an unsuitable potential candidate for the organization to support in the next election. The students created a non-persuasive television ad and podcast, which they unveiled at their press conference.

components rubric

4	3	2	1

research

The students thoroughly explored how an organization has supported candidates and used their position to try to influence voters.	The students explored how an organization has supported candidates and used their position to try to influence voters.	The students partially explored how an organization has supported candidates and used their position to try to influence voters.	The students did not explore how an organization has supported candidates and used their position to try to influence voters.

interview

They conducted a detailed interview with multiple members of their chosen organization.	They conducted a detailed interview with a member of their chosen organization.	They conducted a basic interview with a member of their chosen organization.	They conducted a non-detailed interview with a member of their chosen organization.

propaganda

They examined all of the organization's propaganda as well as the outcomes of those campaigns.	They examined most of the organization's propaganda as well as the outcomes of those campaigns.	They examined some of the organization's propaganda as well as the outcomes of those campaigns.	They examined a few of the organization's propaganda as well as the outcomes of those campaigns.

candidate choice

A well-matched potential candidate for the organization to support in the next election	A suitable potential candidate for the organization to support in the next election	A partially suitable potential candidate for the organization to support in the next election	An unsuitable potential candidate for the organization to support in the next election

ad and podcast

Unique, compelling, and persuasive television ad and podcast, which they unveiled at their press conference	A compelling and persuasive television ad and podcast, which they unveiled at their press conference	A somewhat persuasive television ad and podcast, which they unveiled at their press conference	A non-persuasive television ad and podcast, which they unveiled at their press conference

above

_____
_____
_____

McRel Civics—Standards 20.—Level III—4. Understands the historical and contemporary roles of prominent associations and groups in local, state, and national politics (e.g., historical associations such as abolitionists, suffragists, labor unions, civil rights groups; religious organizations and contemporary associations such as AFL-CIO, National Education Association, Common Cause, League of Women Voters, Greenpeace, National Association for the Advancement of Colored People).

below

_____
_____
_____

above

_____
_____
_____

McREL Civics—Standard 13.—Level III—4. Knows reasons why most political conflict in the United States has generally been less divisive than in many other nations (e.g., a shared respect for the Constitution and its principles, a sense of unity within diversity, willingness to relinquish power when voted out of office, willingness to use the legal system to manage conflicts, opportunities to improve one's economic condition).

below

_____
_____
_____

above

_____
_____
_____

McREL Geography—Standard 4.—Level III—1. Knows the human characteristics of places (e.g., cultural characteristics such as religion, language, politics, technology, family structure, gender; population characteristics; land uses; levels of development).

below

_____
_____
_____

curricular objectives rubric—primary subject

above

_____
_____
_____

McREL Behavioral Studies—Standard 1.—Level III—2. Understands that usually within any society there is broad general agreement on what behavior is "unacceptable," but that the standards used to judge behavior vary for different settings and different subgroups and may change with time and in response to different political and economic conditions.

below

_____
_____
_____

curricular objectives rubric—secondary subjects

above

_____
_____
_____

McREL Technology—Standard 3.—Level III—8. Knows etiquette rules when using the Internet.

below

_____
_____
_____

above

_____
_____
_____

CC W.8.6. Use technology, including the Internet, to produce and publish writing and present the relationships between information and ideas efficiently as well as to interact and collaborate with others.

below

_____
_____
_____

above

_____
_____
_____

CC SL.8.1. Engage effectively in a range of collaborative discussions (one-on-one, in groups, and teacher-led) with diverse partners on Grade 8 topics, texts, and issues, building on others' ideas and expressing their own clearly.

below

_____
_____
_____

above

_____
_____
_____

CC L.8.1. Demonstrate command of the conventions of standard English grammar and usage when writing or speaking.

below

_____
_____
_____

teacher/learner resources

The Most Powerful Political Groups Ever, and Cliques

- http://www.lonympics.co.uk/worldsmostpowpolgroup.htm

The Government of Modern Japan: Interest Groups in Japanese Politics

- http://afe.easia.columbia.edu/at/jp_interest/govigi02.html

Bias and Propaganda

- http://hawaii.hawaii.edu/wwwreading/021R/spring2003/Biasandpropaganda/01.htm

Propaganda Is Not Bias

- http://rhetorica.net/archives/7439.html

Types of Bias

- http://fnopress.com/OWL/owl3.htm

Political Parties as Campaign Organizations

- http://arts.anu.edu.au/sss/abjorensen/pols2067/farrell_webb.pdf

10 Best Political Advertisements of All Time

- http://blog.constitutioncenter.org/10-best-political-advertisements-of-all-time-presidents-edition/

Election Campaigns, Partisan Balance, and the News Media

- http://www.hks.harvard.edu/fs/pnorris/Acrobat/WorldBankReport/Chapter%207%20Semetko.pdf

The Political Impact of Media Bias

- http://elsa.berkeley.edu/~sdellavi/wp/mediabiaswb07-06-25.pdf

The Media Bias in Politics

- http://www.helium.com/knowledge/129423-the-media-bias-in-politics

The Mass Media & Politics: An Analysis of Influence

- http://www.progressiveliving.org/mass_media_and_politics.htm

Do Movie Stars Influence Our Political Opinions?

- http://ezinearticles.com/?Do-Movie-Stars-Influence-Our-Political-Opinions?&id=5310493

The Internet's Influence on Politics and the Election Process

- http://myseniorprojectisablog.wordpress.com/my-essays/the-internets-influence-on-politics-and-the-election-process/

Political Influences

- http://www.123helpme.com/view.asp?id=157515

The Influence of the Media in Politics, Campaigns, and Elections

- http://www.associatedcontent.com/article/443975/the_influence_of_the_media_in_politics.html?cat=9

teacher/learner resources

Interest Groups and Public Opinions

- http://www.google.com.ph/url?sa=t&source=web&cd=2&ved=0CCMQFjAB&url=http%3A%2F%2Fwww.pgcps.org%2F~croom2%2FInterest%2520Groups%2520and%2520Public%2520Opinion.ppt&ei=daolTovGF8OOmQWF96H8CQ&usg=AFQjCNHMaGtqqodGlZmObQqkSJ59pYV82Q

The Role of Interest Groups

- http://www.ait.org.tw/infousa/zhtw/DOCS/Demopaper/dmpaper9.html

Interest Groups Today

- http://xroads.virginia.edu/~ma98/pollklas/thesis/techniques.html

Propaganda

- http://en.wikipedia.org/wiki/Propaganda
- http://themes.pppst.com/propaganda.html

Propaganda Techniques

- http://www.buzzle.com/articles/examples-of-propaganda-techniques.html
- http://www.ehow.com/info_8618687_types-political-propaganda-techniques.html
- http://library.thinkquest.org/C0111500/proptech.htm

American Propaganda: Controlling public opinion in Puerto Rico

- http://www.muralmaster.org/writings/AmerProp/index.html

Propaganda - Propaganda, Diplomacy, and International Public Opinion

- http://www.americanforeignrelations.com/O-W/Propaganda-Propaganda-diplomacy-and-international-public-opinion.html

Propaganda and the Politics of Perception

- http://www.globalresearch.ca/index.php?context=va&aid=5058

The Media's Role in Political Campaigns

- http://www.ericdigests.org/1992-3/role.htm

Political Campaigns and Social Networking

- http://mediaissues.files.wordpress.com/2010/05/political-campaigns-and-social-networking.pdf
- http://trace.tennessee.edu/cgi/viewcontent.cgi?article=2442&context=utk_chanhonoproj

Rise of Modern Propaganda

- http://mason.gmu.edu/~amcdonal/Rise%20of%20Modern%20Propaganda.html

Propaganda or Publicity

- http://html.rincondelvago.com/propaganda-electoral.html

10 Most Evil Propaganda Techniques Used by the Nazis

- http://brainz.org/10-most-evil-propaganda-techniques-used-nazis/

The Most Damaging Propaganda Campaign in History and Its Aimed at You and Me

- http://mandelman.ml-implode.com/2011/05/the-most-damaging-propaganda-campaign-in-history-and-its-aimed-at-you-and-me/

The Differences Between Propaganda & Persuasion

- http://www.ehow.com/info_8635343_differences-between-propaganda-persuasion.html

Media Buying in Political Campaigns: Broadcast Television Remains King

- http://www.campaignsandelections.com/publications/campaign-election/2011/february-2011/Media-Buying-in-Political-Campaigns-Broadcast-Television-Remains-King

5 Ways Political Campaigns Should Measure Social Media

- http://www.associatedcontent.com/article/5652948/5_ways_political_campaigns_should_measure.html?cat=59

8 Tips for Using Social Media for Political Campaigns

- http://www.almostsavvy.com/2011/06/16/8-tips-for-using-social-media-for-political-campaigns/

Using New Media in Political Campaigns

- http://www.slideshare.net/sgranger/using-new-media-in-political-campaigns

Wikipedia: Campaign Advertising

- http://en.wikipedia.org/wiki/Campaign_advertising

Propaganda by Deed

- http://samvak.tripod.com/strikes.html

Media Bias and Influence: Evidence From Newspaper Endorsements

- http://restud.oxfordjournals.org/content/78/3/795.full

Is Winning Newspaper Endorsements Worth a Candidate's Effort?

- http://blogs.wsj.com/capitaljournal/2010/09/15/is-winning-newspaper-endorsements-worth-a-candidate%E2%80%99s-effort/

Caution Against Churches Endorsing Political Candidates

- http://www.gci.org/ethics/caution

Endorsing Candidates. Illegal. How to Do It.

- http://www.blueavocado.org/node/641

Do Candidate Endorsements Matter?

- http://www.onlinecandidate.com/articles/do-candidate-endorsements-matter

questions and ideas to expand this unit

cultivating global digital citizenship

- Based on the research that you have done, choose either an organization or political candidate whose message you believe in and volunteer for them.

- For the next election, create a non-biased information brochure on all the candidates to help others understand the issues and not be influenced by different organizations.

 Personal Responsibility   Global Citizenship   Digital Citizenship   Altruistic Service   Environmental Stewardship

---

Explore propaganda specifically produced by the different political parties. How have their tactics changed through time?

McREL World History—Standard 42.—Level III—2. Understands the ideologies, policies, and governing methods of 20th century totalitarian regimes compared to those of contemporary democracies and absolutist states of earlier centuries.

McREL World History—Standard 42.—Level III—4. Understands ways in which secular ideologies (e.g., nationalism, fascism, communism, materialism) challenged or were challenged by established religions and ethical systems.

Explore how media and technology have affected political campaigns over the past 50 years (beginning with the first televised debate between candidates John F. Kennedy and Richard Nixon).

McREL World History—Standard 44.—Level III—6. Understands the emergence of a global culture (e.g., connections between electronic communications, international marketing, and the rise of a popular "global culture" in the late 20th century; how modern arts have expressed and reflected social transformations, political changes, and how they have been internationalized).

What are the rules and regulations for creating campaign propaganda on behalf of a political candidate?

McREL Civics—Standard 19.—Level III—2. Knows how the public agenda is shaped by political leaders, interest groups, and state and federal courts; and understands how individual citizens can help shape the public agenda (e.g., by joining interest groups or political parties, making presentations at public meetings, writing letters to government officials and to newspapers).

McREL Civics—Standard 19.—Level III—3. Understands the importance of freedom of the press to informed participation in the political system; and understands the influence of television, radio, the press, newsletters, and emerging means of electronic communication on American politics.

questions and ideas to expand this unit

Explore the difference between a newspaper or media outlet and their endorsement of a candidate versus an organization. What kinds of support or propaganda may a newspaper offer versus that which an organization may provide? What are the factors that lead a media outlet to choose a candidate to endorse?

McREL Civics—Standard 19.—Level III—3. Understands the importance of freedom of the press to informed participation in the political system; and understands the influence of television, radio, the press, newsletters, and emerging means of electronic communication on American politics.

Choose a politician who has been in office for more than 20 years. Explore how their campaign messages have changed throughout different campaigns. If the politician has changed levels (for example, moved from state senator to U.S. senator), how has that impacted their propaganda?

McREL Civics—Standard 19.—Level III—6. Understands the opportunities that the media provides for individuals to monitor the actions of their government (e.g., televised broadcasts of proceedings of governmental agencies such as Congress and the courts, public officials' press conferences) and communicate their concerns and positions on current issues (e.g., letters to the editor, talk shows, "op-ed pages," public opinion polls).

Mock Doc

a 21st Century Fluency Project

language arts | grade **10**

10–12 periods

curricular objectives

📖 **CC W.9-10.3.** Write narratives to develop real or imagined experiences or events using effective technique, well-chosen details, and well-structured event sequences.

📖 **CC W.9-10.6.** Use technology, including the Internet, to produce, publish, and update individual or shared writing products, taking advantage of technology's capacity to link to other information and to display information flexibly and dynamically.

📖 **CC SL.9-10.1.** Initiate and participate effectively in a range of collaborative discussions (one-on-one, in groups, and teacher-led) with diverse partners on grades 9–10 topics, texts, and issues, building on others' ideas and expressing their own.

📖 **CC SL.9-10.5.** Make strategic use of digital media (e.g., textual, graphical, audio, visual, and interactive elements) in presentations to enhance understanding of findings, reasoning, and evidence and to add interest.

📖 **CC W.9-10.2.** Write informative/explanatory texts, including the narration of historical events, scientific procedures/ experiments, or technical processes.

📖 **CC RL.9-10.2.**

📖 **CC W.9-10.1.**

📖 **CC L.9-10.1.**

🌐 **McREL Historical Understanding—Standard 2.—Level IV—9.**

(For a full list of standards, see page 196.)

solution fluency

information fluency

creativity fluency

media fluency

collaboration fluency

core concepts matrix

📖 narrative/script writing

📖 documentary production

📖 📐 video editing

📖 📐 digital filmmaking

global digital citizen

* 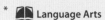 Language Arts   Math   Science   🌐 Social Studies

setting the scene

Students will produce and create a 10- to 20-minute documentary presentation on a topic of their choice.

High Tech: Students will film and edit the production digitally using film equipment and editing software.

Low Tech: Students will do a recording of the script as an audio presentation.

No Tech: Students will perform the script orally using photographs or illustrations for emphasis.

the scenario

Documentaries show a unique side of filmmaking. They demonstrate an intimate knowledge about a particular subject, and it's always something that the creator is passionate or cares very deeply about. Think about all the documentaries you've seen on TV that you really enjoyed. What is it about them that gave you that "wow" factor?

You and a group of friends are taking on a pretty ambitious project. It's time for you to pick a topic or subject that moves, inspires, or excites you and make your own documentary presentation on it. Maybe it's on a special person or place you know or a sport or hobby you like. Maybe it's about a special event or even an incident that will happen or has happened at your school. Maybe it's about a special area of your city with a lot of history. Or you may decide to tackle an even deeper or more challenging subject.

Whatever you decide on, it will take a fun and adventure-filled journey of research and fact-obtaining strategies by your whole team. You will be gathering and analyzing information and data about your topic through reading, writing, photography, recording, interviewing, and video clips. You'll also be looking into the whole exciting process behind bringing a documentary to life, from idea to finished product. This could potentially turn into a field trip–style project where each student group gets a special "research day" to go after the goods on their subject.

Your finished documentary is required to be between 10 and 20 minutes in length. You could choose to film your presentation using a video camera or make a digitally produced one using presentation software, original photos, and video clips. Where possible, include live footage, original photos, and interviews to add dimension and interest. The aim is to bring to your work a feel of being a real masterpiece of documentary making. You are required to include the performed and researched script on the group's chosen subject as a voiceover narration and appearances by all team members involved in the production.

purposely withheld information

Students will need to research the different aspects of documentary filmmaking and production. They'll need to be focusing on how it differs from other filmmaking styles. They will also need to pay strict attention to varying directors' visual styles as they develop one of their own.

the learning process

exploring learner assumptions   1–2 periods

For the beginning of this lesson, discuss and view a sample or samples of documentaries that cover various subjects. Then discuss what students feel was compelling (or even off-putting) about the topics for discussion. Have them direct that same critical eye at how the documentary was styled by the filmmaker and develop a continuing discussion centered on why they feel the directors chose their subject matter and what they might have had to experience or endure to get this film made.

define   1–2 periods

Students have participated in a discussion about the essential question and can now be presented with the outline of the lesson challenge. They are aware that they will be submitting a written definition of the challenges to clarify their understanding of what they are asked to do. They will be working in groups to create an original documentary on a subject they are passionate about or that is important to them. This project may be filmed or created and presented using digital software. Students are required to include their researched and written script in a voiceover format. They also need to incorporate original photography, video footage, and even interviews for maximum effect.

Prerequisites for Progression

Working in groups students have submitted their written definitions of the lesson challenges which include the following:

- outline and draft a script for an original documentary on a subject they are passionate about or that is important to them
- film the documentary using staged sets and actors or render it as an entirely digital production
- include the researched and written script in a voiceover format
- include original photography, video footage, and even interviews for maximum effect
- ensure the finished product is at least 5-8 minutes in length

discover   1–2 periods

Students break up into groups and begin their research on both the art and science behind documentary making. Their aim is to discover and collect information about how topics are chosen and researched and the phases of production that apply. They must think about what is different about making a documentary as opposed to other films. Guide them toward paying careful attention to how subject matter is researched and represented. They need to consider various filmmakers' styles and formatting and even documentaries made on other documentaries. There is a lot of information out there, so students should assemble a very good collection of resource materials to help them in their presentations.

Prerequisites for Progression

Students have done thorough research on documentary filmmaking and its characteristics and concepts. They have collected information and resources on how documentaries are researched and made and are ready to begin visualizing their own.

the learning process

dream

You know you are passionate about something. Now you have a chance to tell others about it and why it's important and worth their attention. You and your friends will use your originally produced documentary as a vehicle for your ideas. So what do you want to make a film about? What is it about this topic that you want to bring to the forefront of viewers' attention and why? How will you use your unique visual style and approach to writing your script that will entertain, inform, and inspire thought and perhaps action? This is your chance to make a truly great and memorable documentary.

Prerequisites for Progression

Students have formed groups and chosen a topic for their documentary. They have visualized and discussed how they want to represent the material from a visual and expository writing perspective.

design

Student groups are now on a quest to research and write about their topic. They will outline and develop their documentary projects using what they have learned in the Discovery phase. They will scout locations if necessary, film their footage, record interviews, take pictures, create original illustrations, and more. They will also outline their scripts and go through editing and revision steps as required. They are required to follow strict deadlines they have created and will hold each other accountable.

Prerequisites for Progression

Student groups have begun the actual creation of their documentary projects and are developing each phase under self-generated deadlines.

deliver—produce

Students put all the finishing touches to their projects by going through any last-minute revisions, additions, or edits. By the end of this phase, they are ready to present their projects in the format to the rest of the class.

Prerequisites for Progression

Each student group has a finished documentary project that has been outlined in the Define phase of the lesson. They have completed revisions and editing at this stage and are ready to present their new projects for assessment.

the learning process

deliver—publish

Each group will present its project to the rest of the class for critique and assessment. The following are some points to consider in each presentation:

- How well have students used their chosen medium (film, animation, slideshow, oral, etc.)?
- How much do they know about their subject matter?
- What is unique or eye-catching about their visual style?
- What kinds of components do they use (photography, illustration, interviews, animations, etc.)?
- What concepts about their subject matter have they chosen to emphasize?

Prerequisites for Progression

Each group has presented its documentary project for the rest of the class and has been given feedback and assessment information.

debrief

Students use this opportunity to reflect on all aspects involved in making a documentary. They discuss what they learned about filmmaking and the new appreciation they have for the processes that bring documentaries to life. Since documentaries are largely made to inform and instruct, have students reflect on their project. How do they feel they represented their subject? Ask them to share what did and did not work. Then have them do the same on the other projects and share what they learned from them. Have them discuss any ideas they may have picked up about the styles and approaches others used in making their presentations.

learning process formative rubric

define

above

Working in groups students have submitted their written definitions of the lesson challenges which include the following:

- outline and draft a script for an original documentary on a subject they are passionate about or that is important to them
- film the documentary using staged sets and actors or render it as an entirely digital production
- include the researched and written script in a voiceover format
- include original photography, video footage, and even interviews for maximum effect
- ensure the finished product is at least 5-8 minutes in length.

below

discover

above

Students have done thorough research on documentary filmmaking and its characteristics and concepts. They have collected information and resources on how documentaries are researched and made and are ready to begin visualizing their own.

below

dream

above

Students have formed groups and chosen a topic for their documentary. They have visualized and discussed how they want to represent the material from a visual and expository writing perspective.

below

learning process formative rubric

design

above

Student groups have begun the actual creation of their documentary projects and are developing each phase under self-generated deadlines.

below

deliver (produce)

above

Each student group has a finished documentary project that has been outlined in the Define phase of the lesson. They have completed revisions and editing at this stage and are ready to present their new projects for assessment.

below

deliver (publish)

above

Each group has presented their documentary project for the rest of the class and has been given feedback and assessment information.

below

4

The group members have chosen a topic of genuine interest for them for their documentary. They showed evidence of extensive research on their subject matter. They incorporated a variety of different media in their presentation for interest and appeal. The overall project flowed well and was structured well. Their documentary script was well written and illustrated the subject. They answered all questions clearly and accurately.

3

The group members have chosen a topic of interest to them for their documentary. They showed evidence of research on their subject matter. They incorporated different media in their presentation for interest and appeal. The overall project flowed and was structured well. Their documentary script was mostly well written and illustrated the subject. They answered most questions clearly and accurately.

2

The group members have chosen a topic they are somewhat interested in for their documentary. They showed evidence of some research on their subject matter. They incorporated some different media in their presentation for interest and appeal. The overall project struggled in its flow and structure. Their documentary script was somewhat well written and briefly illustrated the subject. They answered some questions clearly and accurately.

1

The group members have not chosen a topic of interest to them for their documentary. They showed evidence of little research on their subject matter. They incorporated few different media in their presentation for interest and appeal. The overall project lacked flow and was loosely structured. Their documentary script was poorly written and vaguely illustrated the subject. They answered few questions clearly and accurately.

components rubric

	4	**3**	**2**	**1**
topic	The group members have chosen a topic of genuine interest for them for their documentary.	The group members have chosen a topic of interest to them for their documentary.	The group members have chosen a topic they are somewhat interested in for their documentary.	The group members have not chosen a topic of interest to them for their documentary.
research	They showed evidence of extensive research on their subject matter.	They showed evidence of research on their subject matter.	They showed evidence of some research on their subject matter.	They showed evidence of little research on their subject matter.
media	They incorporated a variety of different media in their presentation for interest and appeal.	They incorporated a variety of different media in their presentation for interest and appeal.	They incorporated some different media in their presentation for interest and appeal.	They incorporated few different media in their presentation for interest and appeal.
flow and structure	The overall project flowed well and was structured well.	The overall project flowed and was structured well.	The overall project struggled in its flow and structure.	The overall project lacked flow and was loosely structured.
script	Their documentary script was well written and illustrated the subject.	Their documentary script was mostly well written and illustrated the subject.	Their documentary script was somewhat well written and briefly illustrated the subject.	Their documentary script was poorly written and vaguely illustrated the subject.
discussion	They answered all questions clearly and accurately.	They answered most questions clearly and accurately.	They answered some questions clearly and accurately.	They answered few questions clearly and accurately.

curricular objectives rubric—primary subject

above

CC W.9-10.3. Write narratives to develop real or imagined experiences or events using effective technique, well-chosen details, and well-structured event sequences.

below

above

CC W.9-10.6. Use technology, including the Internet, to produce, publish, and update individual or shared writing products, taking advantage of technology's capacity to link to other information and to display information flexibly and dynamically.

below

above

CC SL.9-10.1. Initiate and participate effectively in a range of collaborative discussions (one-on-one, in groups, and teacher-led) with diverse partners on Grades 9–10 topics, texts, and issues, building on others' ideas and expressing their own.

below

above

CC SL.9-10.5. Make strategic use of digital media (e.g., textual, graphical, audio, visual, and interactive elements) in presentations to enhance understanding of findings, reasoning, and evidence and to add interest.

below

curricular objectives rubric—primary subject

above

_____
_____
_____
_____

CC W.9-10.2. Write informative/explanatory texts, including the narration of historical events, scientific procedures, experiments, or technical processes.

below

_____
_____
_____
_____

above

_____
_____
_____
_____

CC RL.9-10.2. Determine a theme or central idea of a text and analyze in detail its development over the course of the text, including how it emerges and is shaped and refined by specific details; provide an objective summary of the text.

below

_____
_____
_____
_____

above

_____
_____
_____
_____

CC W.9-10.1. Write arguments to support claims in an analysis of substantive topics or texts, using valid reasoning and relevant and sufficient evidence.

below

_____
_____
_____
_____

above

_____
_____
_____
_____

CC L.9-10.1. Demonstrate command of the conventions of standard English grammar and usage when writing or speaking.

below

_____
_____
_____
_____

above

McREL Historical Understanding—Standard 2.—Level IV—9. Analyzes how specific historical events would be interpreted differently based on newly uncovered records and/or information.

below

above

McREL Art Connections—Standard 1.—Level IV—2. Knows how characteristics of the arts vary within a particular historical period or style and how these characteristics relate to ideas, issues, or themes in other disciplines.

below

above

McREL Arts and Communication—Standard 3.—Level IV—7. Understands how personal experience can influence interpretations of different art forms.

below

above

McREL Arts and Communication—Standard 1.—Level IV—4. Uses production concepts and techniques (e.g., auditioning, directing, producing, scheduling) for various media (e.g., theatre, film, television, electronic media).

below

above

McREL Geography—Standard 6.—Level IV—1. Understands why places and regions are important to individual human identity and as symbols for unifying or fragmenting society (e.g., sense of belonging, attachment, or rootedness; symbolic meaning of places such as Jerusalem as a holy city for Muslims, Christians, and Jews).

below

above

McREL Historical Understanding—Standard 2.—Level IV—12. Knows how to evaluate the credibility and authenticity of historical sources.

below

above

McREL Historical Understanding—Standard 2.—Level IV—13. Evaluates the validity and credibility of different historical interpretations.

below

curricular objectives rubric—secondary subjects

above

McREL Theatre—Standard 1.—Level IV—1. Constructs imaginative scripts that convey story and meaning to an audience.

below

above

McREL Theatre—Standard 6.—Level IV—1. Understands how similar themes are treated in drama from various cultures and historical periods.

below

above

McREL Technology—Standard 2.—Level IV—2. Knows how to import and export text, data, and graphics between software programs.

below

Articles on Offending Viewers

- http://www.guardian.co.uk/media/organgrinder/2009/jun/24/jana-bennett-bbc
- http://simchafisher.wordpress.com/2010/07/07/if-the-movie-offends-thee/
- http://www.guardian.co.uk/media/organgrinder/2009/jun/24/bbc-standards-report-blog
- http://mediaandreligion482.blogspot.com/2010/09/are-screenwriters-religious.html

Behind-the-Scenes Documentary

- http://www.themotionfactory.com/index.php?option=com_content&view=article&id=28:
  behind-the-scenes-documentary&catid=3:project-examples&Itemid=3

The Five Elements of Documentary

- http://www.dvworkshops.com/newsletters/fiveelements.html

Example: Surf's Up—The Making of an Animated Documentary

- http://www.imageworks.com/ipax/docs/Siggraph2007SurfsUpCourseNotes.pdf

How to Write a Documentary Script

- http://portal.unesco.org/ci/en/files/24367/11757852251documentary_script.pdf/
  documentary_script.pdf

Mockumentary

- http://www.wowessays.com/dbase/ac3/ena134.shtml

Have Movies Affected Our Culture?

- http://www.helium.com/items/2092428-have-movies-affected-our-culture

History of Film

- http://en.wikipedia.org/wiki/History_of_film

The Importance of Short Film: Then and Now

- http://www.timeimage.org.uk/feature_the_importance_of_short_film.html

Independent Film Strategies

- http://www.atarh.com/martini-quickshot-creator-storyboard-strategies-for-independent-
  films.html
- http://www.filmproposals.com/Attract-Film-Investors.html
- http://www.peterbroderick.com/writing/writing/ultralowbudgetmoviemaking.html

Top 50 Documentaries of the Decade (With Trailer)

- http://www.thedocumentaryblog.com/index.php/2010/01/05/the-documentary-blogs-top-
  25-documentaries-of-the-decade/

Best Documentaries of the Decade

- http://www.pastemagazine.com/blogs/lists/2009/11/the-25-best-documentaries-of-the-decade-2000-2009.html
- http://theplaylist.blogspot.com/2009/12/playlists-best-documentaries-of-decade.html
- http://popcultureninja.com/2010/06/14/top-25-documentaries-of-the-last-decade/
- http://documentaries.about.com/od/recommendeddocumentaries/tp/Best_Documentaries_of_the_2000s.htm
- http://www.incilin.com/?p=2699

questions and ideas to expand this unit

cultivating global digital citizenship

💻 👤 Create a contest for best student-produced documentary on a subject of importance to the school or environment.

💔 💻 👤 Support local filmmakers covering issues of interest to them and the community.

💔 🌿 👤 Invite filmmakers as guest speakers to the class, or develop and produce a special project with them and their crew to bring attention to an issue of appeal and importance.

💻 👤 Provide workshops on filmmaking and documentaries to other students, and place information/developments on a web project to share and collaborate with other schools in different districts or countries.

 Personal Responsibility
 Global Citizenship
 Digital Citizenship
 Altruistic Service
 Environmental Stewardship

How do the attitudes and approaches of directors potentially offend or alienate certain viewers?

McREL Thinking and Reasoning—Standard 2.—Level IV—6. Understands that people sometimes reach false conclusions either by applying faulty logic to true statements or by applying valid logic to false statements.

McREL Thinking and Reasoning—Standard 2.—Level IV—8. Understands that logic can be used to test how well any general rule works.

Why have films become so important in our culture, from the first moving pictures to present day?

McREL Visual Arts—Standard 2.—Level IV—1. Understands how visual, spatial, temporal, and functional values of artworks are tempered by culture and history.

McREL Visual Arts—Standard 4.—Level IV—1. Knows a variety of historical and cultural contexts regarding characteristics and purposes of works of art.

What are the strategies that amateur or lesser known filmmakers need to follow to get their short or independent films promoted and seen in a big-budget competitive market?

McREL Business Education—Standard 15.—Level IV—2. Knows that entrepreneurship relates to the capacity to take responsibility for one's own future, to initiate creative ideas, develop them, and to carry them through into action in a determined manner.

Discuss some of the so-called greatest documentaries of the past 10 years.

McREL Art Connections—Standard 1.—Level IV—3. Understands how elements, materials, technologies, artistic processes (e.g., imagination, craftsmanship), and organizational principles (e.g., unity and variety, repetition and contrast) are used in similar and distinctive ways in the various art forms.

McREL Arts and Communication—Standard 2.—Level IV—8. Critiques art works in terms of the historical and cultural context in which they were created (e.g., critiquing the musical compositions of Mozart in terms of other musical compositions of the Classic era).

References and Resources

Anderson, L. & Krathwohl, D. (2001). *A taxonomy for learning, teaching and assessing—A revision of Bloom's taxonomy of educational objectives.* New York: Longman.

Adams, S. (1996). *The Dilbert principle: A cubicle's-eye view of bosses, meetings, management fads & other workplace afflictions.* New York: Harper Collins.

Bauerlein, M. (2008). *The dumbest generation: How the digital age stupefies young Americans and jeopardizes our future (Or, don't trust anyone under 30).* New York: Tarcher.

Buck Institute for Education. (2003). *Project based learning handbook: A guide to standards-focused project-based learning for middle and high school teachers* (2nd ed.). Novato, CA.

Burmark, L. (2002). *Visual literacy: Learn to see, see to learn.* New York: ASCD.

Canton, J. (2006). *The extreme future: The top trends that will reshape the world for the next 5, 10, and 20 years.* New York: Penguin.

Carter, R. (2009). *The human brain book: An illustrated guide to its structure, function and disorders.* London: Dorling Kindersley.

Crossman, W. (2004). *VIVO: The coming age of talking computers.* Oakland, CA: Regent Press.

Dryden, G. & Vos, J. (2009). *Unlimited: The new learning revolution and the seven keys to unlock it.* Auckland, New Zealand: The Learning Web.

Florida, R. (2002). *The rise of the creative class: And how it's transforming work, leisure, community, and everyday life.* New York: Basic Books.

Friedman, T. (2005). *The world is flat: A brief history of the twenty-first century.* New York: Farrar, Straus and Giroux.

Friedman, T. (2008). *Hot, flat, and crowded: Why we need a green revolution and how it can renew America.* New York: Farrar, Straus and Giroux.

Gardner, H. (1983). *Frames of mind: Theories of multiple intelligences.* New York: Basic Books.

Garreau, J. (2005). *Radical evolution: The promise and peril of enhancing our minds, bodies—and what it means to be human.* New York: Random House.

Glasser, W. (1998). *The quality school.* New York: Harper.

Glatthorn, A. (1987). *Curriculum Leadership* (Good Year Book). New York: Scott Foresman & Co., p. 237.

Godin, S. (2011). *Linchpin: are you indispensible?* New York: Portfolio Trade.

Goodstein, A. (2007). *Totally wired: What teens and tweens are really doing online.* New York: St. Martin's Griffin.

Harvard Business Review. (2004). *Breakthrough ideas for 2004.* Cambridge, MA: Harvard Business School Publishing Company.

Hill, J. (2008, October). YouTube surpasses Yahoo! as world's #2 search engine. *TG Daily*, October 17. Retrieved from http://www.tgdaily.com/trendwatch-features/39777-youtube-surpasses-yahoo-as-world's-2-search-engine

Hirsch, E. D. (1988). *Cultural literacy: What every American needs to know.* New York: Vintage Books.

Jensen, E. (1997). *Completing the puzzle: The brain-compatible approach to learning.* Del Mar, CA: The Brain Store.

Jensen, E. (2008). *Super teaching: Over 1000 practical strategies.* Press, p..42. Thousand Oaks, CA: Corwin.

Johnson, S. (2005). *Everything bad is good for you: How today's popular culture is actually making us smarter.* New York: Riverhead.

Jukes, I., McCain, T., & Crockett L. (2010). *Living on the future edge: Windows on tomorrow.* Kelowna, BC: 21st Century Fluency Project.

Kandel, E. (2006). *In search of memory: The emergence of a new science of mind.* London: W.W. Norton.

Kelly, F., McCain, T., & Jukes, I. (2008). *Teaching the digital generation: No more cookie-cutter high schools.* Thousand Oaks, CA: Corwin.

Kolb, L. (2008). *Toys to tools: Connecting student cell phones to education.* Eugene, OR: ISTE.

Kurzweil, R. (2005). *The singularity is near: When humans transcend biology.* New York: Viking Press.

Marzano, R. (1998). *A theory-based meta-analysis of research on instruction.* Aurora, CO: Mid-Continent Regional Educational Laboratory.

Marzano, R. (2003). *What works in schools: Translating research into action.* ASCD: Alexandria, VA.

McCain, T. (2005). *Teaching for tomorrow: Teaching content and problem-solving skills.* Thousand Oaks, CA: Corwin.

McCain, T. & Jukes, I. (2000). *Windows on the future: Education in the age of technology.* Thousand Oaks, CA: Corwin.

McLuhan, M. (1964). *Understanding media: The extensions of man.* Boston: MIT Press.

Mead, M. (1968). *Continuities in cultural evolution.* New Haven, CT: Yale University Press.

Medina, J. (2008). *Brain rules: 12 principles for surviving and thriving at work, home, and school.* Seattle, WA: Pear Press.

Naisbitt, J. (2006). *Mind set!: Reset your thinking and see the future.* New York: HarperBusiness.

Nielsen, J. & Loranger, H. (2006). *Prioritizing web usability.* Berkley: New Riders Press

Neisser, U., & Hyman, Y. (1999). *Memory observed: Remembering in natural contexts.* (2nd ed.). New York: Worth Publishing.

Peters, T. & Waterman, R. H. (2004). *In search of excellence: Lessons from America's best-run companies.* New York: Harper Collins.

Pink, D. (2001). *Free agent nation—The future of working for yourself.* Chicago: Business Plus.

Pink, D. (2005). *A whole new mind: Moving from the information age to the conceptual age.* New York: Riverhead.

Prensky, M. (2006). *Don't bother me mom—I'm learning.* St. Paul, MN: Paragon House.

Prensky, M. (2010). *Teaching digital natives—Partnering for real learning.* Thousand Oaks, CA: Corwin.

Rae-Dupree, J. (2008). Let computers compute. It's the age of the right brain. *New York Times,* April 6. Retrieved from http://www.nytimes.com/2008/04/06/technology/06unbox.html

Reeves, T. (1998). The impact of media and technology on schools. Bertelsmann Foundation. itech1.coe.uga.edu/~treeves/edit6900/BertelsmannReeves98.pdf

Richardson, W. (2008). *Blogs, wikis, podcasts, and other powerful web tools for classrooms.* Thousand Oaks, CA: Corwin.

Rideout, V. & Hamel, E. (2006). *The media family: Electronic media in the lives of infants, toddlers, preschoolers, school age children and their parents.* Chestnut Hill, MA: Boston College.

Shirky, C. (2008). *Here comes everybody: The power of organizing with organizations.* New York: Penguin Press.

Singleton, D. & Lengyl, Z. (1995). *The age factor in second language acquisition.* Bristol, UK: Multilingual Matters Ltd.

Small, G. & Vorgon, G. (2008). *iBrain: Surviving the technological alteration of the modern mind.* New York: Harper Collins.

Sousa, D. (2005). *How the brain learns.* Thousand Oaks, CA: Corwin.

Tapscott, D. (2008). *Wikinomics: How mass collaboration changes everything.* New York: McGraw-Hill.

Tapscott, D. (2009). *Grown up digital: How the net generation is changing your world.* New York: McGraw-Hill.

Trilling, B. & Fadel, C. (2009). *21st century skills: Learning for life in our times.* San Francisco: Jossey-Bass.

Wilson, W. (1909, January). *The meaning of a liberal education.* New York: High School Teachers Association Address.

Wong, G. (2011, May). YouTube: More than 48 hours of video uploaded every minute. *Übergizmo,* May 25. Retrieved from http://www.ubergizmo.com/2011/05/youtube-more-than-48-hours-minute/

Wurman, R. S. (2002). *Information anxiety.* New York: Hayden.

Zemke, R. (1985). *Computer literacy needs assessment—A trainer's guide.* New York: Addison Wesley.

Zittrain, J. (2008). *The future of the Internet—And how to stop it.* New York: Yale University Press.

Index

21st Century Fluency Project

Getting it Right

Aligning Technology Initiatives
for Measuarable Student Results

Coming in Fall 2011!

The changes we are facing in the world today are staggering, and this is especially true in education. But if you take time to align your initiatives with your intended learning goals, every minute spent planning and questioning will save an hour at the implementation stage, not to mention huge sums of money.

That is the whole idea behind our upcoming book, *Getting it Right: Aligning Technology Initiatives for Measurable Student Results.* This informative and revealing book is designed to help teachers, educational leaders, and decision makers wade through the complexities of technology planning. It provides an overview of how you can address state or provincial standards, improve test scores, meet your curricular requirements, foster relevant staff development, and provide measurable accountability for expenditures. At the same time, we'll show you how you can ensure that your students are effectively equipped with the skills and knowledge they will need to cope with the new realities of the 21st century.

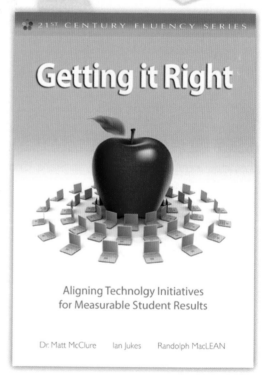

www.fluency21.com